Silver AND
THE FIRST
NEW DEAL

Silver AND
THE FIRST
NEW DEAL

BY JOHN A. BRENNAN

UNIVERSITY OF NEVADA PRESS

RENO · NEVADA 1969

University of Nevada Press   •   Reno, Nevada
© 1969 University of Nevada Press
Library of Congress Catalog Card Number 68–56289

Designed by Wolfgang Lederer
Printed in the United States of America

SBN 87417–023–0

Acknowledgments

Many persons have, directly or indirectly, assisted me in my study of the silver movement. Their contributions are gratefully acknowledged in the following résumé, which outlines the successive steps leading to this publication.

Professor Robert G. Athearn of the University of Colorado History Department encouraged my doctoral studies and approved a study of the Senate Silver Bloc; as my mentor he obtained departmental assistantships. A political-scientist colleague, Professor Dayton M. McKean, while Dean of the Graduate School, approved a University Fellowship to support my travel needs. Thereafter, dozens of archivists and librarians in thirteen western states, Washington, D.C., and Hyde Park, New York, provided the basic source materials upon my arrival at their repositories. Back in Boulder, Colorado, several fellow graduate students helped me to persevere despite first-draft labor pains, and in 1964 Carl Jackson gave me respite through employment as curator of the University of Colorado Western Historical Collection.

Dr. Ralph E. Ellsworth, Director of Libraries, granted me leave-of-absence time during the 1966–1967 academic year to complete the final drafts of the dissertation. That winter, direction by Professors Athearn and Howard L. Scamehorn, also of the Department of History, sharpened the focus of my writings, while two loyal friends, Mr. and Mrs. James L. Mudge, listened sympathetically to my complaints, typed, proofread, and generally eased my trials.

Still others aided in making this book. Professor Russell R. Elliott and other critical readers of the University of Nevada recommended publication; Robert Laxalt, director of the University of Nevada Press, approved; any readability found herein results from N. M. Cady's editorial staff. Finally, my wife Ann's eagle-eyed galley-proofing and indexing talents are much appreciated, as is her encouragement of my research interests even when they take time away from our partnership.

J.A.B.

Boulder, Colorado
July, 1969

Contents

1 The Revival of the Silver Issue

SILVER money has frequently become involved in domestic political controversy. The white metal was equal to gold as a medium of exchange and as a standard of value until 1873, when Congress eliminated the standard silver dollar from coinage and limited its legal-tender status. In subsequent years of intense monetary agitation, this action—taken by Congress as a routine measure important only to perfect the coinage system—was depicted as the "Crime of '73" by those who believed that the denial of silver's equality with gold was a direct attack upon the common people.

The recurring silver controversy reflected both much larger issues and the demands of special interests. Perennially, the mining industry sought to stabilize demand for its silver, and the banking industry strove to protect the value of its money. Meanwhile, millions of rural citizens in the developing West and South periodically became enraged over acute shortages of credit and cash. They were convinced that "the money trust" must be causing these gyrations for its own benefit and that it probably was also responsible for demonetizing silver. Lingering doubts over these accusations were erased by well-established economic facts. During the late nineteenth century, prices for staple crops and silver declined when the dollar's value appreciated in terms of gold. Thus, farmers blamed the monetary system when their productive efforts brought them large debts and but few of the rewards available to their urban countrymen.

Monetary crises beset American politics and persistently disturbed the financial system during three decades of the late nine-

1

teenth and early twentieth centuries. The silver issue erupted during this time. Because of agitation for monetary inflation and higher prices for the white metal in the seventies, Congress adopted the Bland-Allison Act of 1878. That measure authorized the Treasury Department to buy from two to four million dollars worth of silver each month and to coin this metal into dollars. The act also permitted the issue of silver certificates in lieu of coin and redeemable in gold. While this compromise fell short of demands for free and unlimited coinage, its terms satisfied most miners, farmers, and bankers at the time.

In 1890, Congress doubled its mandate to the Treasury through the Sherman Silver Purchase Act. This law required purchase of 4.5 million ounces per month, an amount equivalent to the total domestic production, and continued the redemption of silver certificates for either silver or gold. Bankers, thereafter, became distrustful of federal finances and rapidly exchanged the certificates for gold. This trend generated a crisis which prompted repeal in 1893 of the Sherman Silver Purchase Act's purchasing clause. Elimination of silver buying failed to ease the financial disruption, however, and instead began the series of events that produced William Jennings Bryan's unsuccessful "free silver" campaign in 1896.

The great depression in the thirties revived agitation for remonetization, monetary inflation, and control of the dollar's value. Again, this sentiment led to new silver purchase legislation. Actually, proposals such as these had reappeared early in the twenties—each intending to raise the metal's price and to restore its status. Among them were plans authorizing the mints to coin all silver bullion presented to them; others called for an international conference to achieve greater use of silver as money; and others assured limited federal purchases in exchange for silver certificates.

Producers persistently sought legislation requiring the Treasury to buy the white metal. This was a direct answer to their problems, and its precedents, including the Bland-Allison Act, the Sherman Silver Purchase Act, and the Pittman Act of 1918, were useful tactical weapons. After completion of purchases under the latter measure in 1923, mineowners and their representatives in the United States Senate began a drive for new legislation. The seven most affected states, represented by concerned senators, were, in output order: Utah, Idaho, Montana, Arizona, Nevada, Colorado, and New Mexico.

The senators from these states played a prominent role in the attempt to remonetize silver—to restore it to the value it had before the "Crime of '73." Beginning with the drive for new legislation in 1923, efforts continued throughout several decades. While the senators frequently disagreed on the proper course of action, all of them pursued their goal vigorously in the belief that remonetization was essential to protect the mining states' economies. The Silver Bloc proved to be an important avenue through which several of these men worked.

The leaders of the Silver Bloc were three uncommon men who shared common interests: William E. Borah of Idaho, Burton K. Wheeler of Montana, and Key Pittman of Nevada. As young lawyers, they had all succumbed to the urge to "go west," and had become identified with the development of mining in their adopted states. For the remainder of their lives, they sought to assist the western mining industry.

Borah arrived in Idaho in 1890 and quickly became a respected attorney at law. Time and events steadily enhanced his reputation. Shortly after his election to the Senate in 1906, he won national fame as state prosecutor in the trial of William D. Haywood, a labor leader accused of complicity in the murder of a former governor of Idaho. In Washington, Borah specialized in foreign policy questions and eventually became a leading Republican spokesman in that field. His reelections became formalities; his majority increased each time until in 1930 it reached 80 percent. Borah's biographer has asserted that his subject's unusual independence of thought and action found acceptance even among his opponents because he was generally judged to be morally unimpeachable.[1]

Wheeler became involved in Montana's tumultuous politics soon after he moved to that state. Like Borah, Wheeler's initial prominence sprang from his role as prosecutor. He was United

3

States District Attorney at Butte from 1913 to 1918; following election to the Senate four years later, he became prosecutor for a select committee investigating the Justice Department. The national acclaim that resulted won for Wheeler the Independent Progressive party's vice-presidential nomination in 1924. A decade later, he struggled with Franklin D. Roosevelt over domestic and foreign policies. His opposition to American policy before the attack on Pearl Harbor probably caused his defeat in the 1946 primary.[2]

Key Pittman arrived in Nevada in 1902. Previously he had prospected for gold in Yukon Territory following his legal education in Seattle. His practice of mining law flourished during Tonopah, Nevada's, bonanza years. In that period Pittman was also active in Nevada's Democratic party. In 1912 the state's small population elected him to the Senate.[3] Later years provided them with little cause for regret, for his interests were those of his constituents—particularly in his defense of the mining industry. Pittman was the Senate's most industrious and successful proponent of legislation to help silver producers.

Nevada's other senators shared Pittman's ardor for silver. Republican Tasker L. Oddie, a former governor of Nevada who had made and lost his fortune in the Tonopah mines, served from 1921 to 1933, losing his seat to Democrat Patrick A. McCarran, a colorful jurist and Pittman's bitter rival for control of Nevada's Democratic party.[4] Their feud flared in the Senate, where McCarran found many faults in Pittman's legislative proposals on silver.

The senators from Utah also were faithful to silver interests. The senior man was Republican Reed Smoot, a Mormon apostle first elected in 1903 but not seated until four years later because of objections rooted in the polygamy issue. Smoot remained in Washington until defeated in 1932 by Elbert D. Thomas, a liberal Democrat and professor of political science at the University of Utah. Smoot's national prominence arose from his chairmanship of the Senate Committee on Finance and his sponsorship of the nationalistic Smoot-Hawley Tariff of 1930. Thomas, on the other hand, was an internationally-minded supporter of the New Deal. Democrat William H. King won his seat in 1916 and retained it until his anti-New Deal posture cost him the 1940 election.[5] King was more closely identified with the silver interests than either of his Utah colleagues.

The senators from Colorado, New Mexico, and Arizona also supported the silver agitation, but less actively than their associates in the Silver Bloc. Of these legislators, Colorado's Alva B. Adams, a Democrat elected in 1932, and Carl Hayden of Arizona, a Democrat elected in 1926, displayed the greatest interest in silver legislation.[6]

The Bloc's legislative demands were ultimately met by the Silver Purchase Act of 1934. That measure partially restored the white metal's monetary status, causing a temporary increase in prices. Its adoption resulted from sustained and coordinated action by agricultural as well as mining interests in response to the great depression.[7]

The mining industry experienced economic difficulties long before the onset of depression. After 1920, supplies of silver increasingly outran the demand. Production increased because it was largely a by-product of mining for copper, lead, and zinc, but consumption failed to rise commensurably because of demonetization in Europe and Asia. In the twenties, returns to the market of such metal totaled approximately 300 million ounces, or 10 percent more than the world's annual production in earlier years when the demand for base metals was very strong.[8]

Excess supplies of silver in the twenties brought declining prices. These dropped from $1.38 per ounce in November of 1919 to approximately eighty cents per ounce six months later. In the following year, prices continued to fall until they stabilized between sixty-two and seventy-four cents per ounce, the range which had been usual before World War I. These prices soon eliminated many marginal silver mines because production costs remained above prewar levels.[9]

By grace of the Pittman Act, silver producers had a brief respite from sinking prices. The act authorized the Treasury to buy silver from domestic production at $1.00 per ounce, replacing bullion sold at that price to India for war purposes. This acquisition began in 1920 after world prices had fallen below $1.00

per ounce.[10] In reaction to declining prices on the world market, decisions by Great Britain and Holland to reduce their stocks of silver, and the prospect that Treasury purchases would be ended, producers turned to the western senators for help in soliciting aid from the federal government.[11]

In September of 1922, more than a year before purchases under the Pittman Act would be fulfilled, mining industry leaders met with a group of senators. They gathered in the offices of Key Pittman of Nevada to explore the existing and prospective problems facing producers. In addition to Pittman, the senators included Samuel D. Nicholson and Lawrence C. Phipps of Colorado, Thomas J. Walsh of Montana, Frank R. Gooding of Idaho, William H. King of Utah, and Tasker L. Oddie of Nevada. The businessmen were J. F. Callbreath, secretary of the American Mining Congress, H. N. Lawrie, general manager of the American Gold and Silver Institute, and Ravenal Macbeth, president of the Idaho Mine Operators' Association.[12]

The legislators and mining leaders discussed varied means to improve the prospects for silver. Only a general outline of their conversations was recorded; they mentioned several possible actions which later became focal points of agitation. Pittman suggested that the federal government loan silver bullion to China to strengthen its silver standard, replacing the metal from domestic production. King advocated a conference to establish a ratio for the value of silver to gold by international agreement and to secure a greater use of silver for monetary purposes. Lawrie urged that steps be taken to break the alleged British control over world market prices for the white metal and suggested a way to stimulate demand in India.[13] The immediate result of this meeting was to focus the senators' attention on the problems confronting the silver mining industry.

In 1923, the western senators worked closely with the silver producers. Both groups were surprised and provoked by a Treasury Department announcement that silver purchases would be completed several months earlier than previously announced. Reacting swiftly, the legislators gained authority for a Commission of Gold and Silver Inquiry composed of five of their number:

Oddie, Pittman, Walsh, Gooding, and Thomas Sterling of South Dakota. The commission was authorized to investigate "the causes of the depressed condition of the gold and silver industry in the United States."[14] Using this authority, Pittman launched an investigation into the Treasury's action under the act bearing his name.[15]

In September of 1923, at Reno, Nevada, leaders of the domestic mining industry assembled at the request of the Senate's Commission of Gold and Silver Inquiry. The purpose of this gathering was twofold: it encouraged producers to show their displeasure over the Treasury's handling of purchases under the Pittman Act,[16] and it facilitated development of an organization representing the silver mining industry. Pittman urged the producers to form an export association to control and finance the withholding of silver from foreign markets. He asserted that such an organization would give small producers a voice in determining prices for their products and that it would ease their credit problems.[17]

Several major producers forcefully rejected Pittman's call for an export association. Cornelius F. Kelley, president of the Anaconda Copper Mining Company, predicted that financial problems would overwhelm such an organization, as had nearly been the case with the Copper Export Association a few years earlier. Furthermore, he argued that the industry was unable to regulate its output and that the American companies could not control the total supply of silver sufficiently to exact higher prices. Francis H. Brownell, first vice-president of the American Smelting and Refining Company, also opposed Pittman's proposal, explaining that the most pressing need was to reverse the decline in use of monetary silver. He therefore urged the formation of a producers' association to encourage greater consumption by industry and government.[18]

Thereafter the silver producers charted their own course. They appointed a committee to determine the type of organization which would best suit their needs. It met at New York's Waldorf-Astoria Hotel in November, 1923, to hear from representatives of each segment of the industry. The committee's membership

7

controlled approximately 90 percent of the domestic silver supply, and its chairman, Cornelius F. Kelley, represented the nation's largest producer at that time. One of the persons invited to speak, C. W. Harman, the president of the Sterling Silverware Manufacturers' Association, also opposed demands for an export association.[19] After three days of consultation the committee rejected the export association idea, preferring a producers' association.

In August, 1924, the producers met at Salt Lake City and established the American Silver Producers' Association.[20] Its declared purpose was "to prosecute any and all lines of activity which may subserve and promote the welfare of the silver mining industry." The following year the association became a nonprofit corporation chartered in Utah with headquarters in the offices of its president, W. Mont. Ferry, at Salt Lake City.[21] He was vice-president and general manager of the Silver King Coalition Mining Company, a profitable, medium-sized organization owning numerous silver-lead mines at Park City, Utah.[22] The association's secretary-treasurer, Henry N. Rives, was also secretary-treasurer of the Nevada Mine Operators' Association. Membership included approximately fifty companies,[23] but it was dominated by American Smelting's Francis H. Brownell. He was one of the four members of the executive committee that operated from New York City. The association remained active until 1933, when a split between western and eastern leaders brought about its demise.[24]

After 1924, Brownell emerged as the silver producers' most articulate spokesman. He was well prepared for this task. After graduating from Brown University in 1888, he studied at the Columbia University Law School from 1888 through 1890, and soon became a leading attorney at Everett, Washington, during its early "boom" period. Subsequently, he was named legal counsel and later president of the Federal Mining and Smelting Company, a western subsidiary of American Smelting. In time Brownell advanced to general counsel of the parent company, became a vice-president in 1917, first vice-president two years later, board chairman in 1930, and chief executive officer early in the following decade.[25]

Despite Brownell's capacity for leadership, the association proved ineffective, primarily because its members had conflicting goals. A majority of the mining companies involved operated in the western states and had properties only in those regions. However, the major firms, headquartered in New York and Boston, had smelting and refining operations as well as mines, and possessed foreign subsidiaries and fabricating facilities.[26] The policies beneficial to the large eastern firms frequently were opposed by their small competitors, consequently leading to either inaction or a restraint that prevented substantial accomplishment.

Brownell's attitude toward Charles S. Thomas demonstrated the producers' conflict of interests. Thomas was the association's representative in Washington and a former senator from Colorado. As a lawyer he had represented both Anaconda and American Smelting, but he also shared the beliefs and aspirations of the small mine operators in the West. Thomas suggested that silver men should adopt a rationale similar to that of the farmers who were asserting their need of "direct contributions" from the federal government "whereby prices of their products may be . . . kept at a level about the cost of production."[27] The former senator believed that producers should cooperate with the leaders of farm organizations for their mutual benefit. However, Brownell rejected his proposal because "any such reciprocal endorsement would . . . savor too strongly of a combined raid upon the Treasury, of special interests." He also said that proposals on silver should be advanced on their own merits.[28] Furthermore, Brownell rebuffed Thomas' request that the Producers' Association cooperate with organized labor.

> After talking with my associates, we feel that probably the American silver industry had better not lay itself under obligation to the American Federation of Labor. . . . If they should help us, the natural implication is that the silver industry should return the compliment sometime, and it might be more or less embarrassing to do so.[29]

Brownell's refusal to join with other interest groups weakened the association's drive to secure favorable treatment in Washington. None of its endeavors was successful. For nearly five years, Thomas and Pittman sought to reverse the Treasury's decision not to purchase at $1.00 per ounce the silver allocated to subsidiary coinage under the authority of the Pittman Act. The department had acquired fifteen million ounces at the market price, and it easily thwarted pressures, legislative moves, and court action undertaken by the association.[30] Moreover, Senator Oddie met with similar results in his efforts in 1930 to interest the secretary of Commerce in the problems of the silver producers. That official, Thomas P. Lamont, said he could do nothing about the mineowners' difficulties because the control of consumption was impossible and the control of production was impracticable. He insisted that "the price of silver must eventually be determined by economic laws."[31]

Such replies went virtually unchallenged because the industry lacked unity and public support, although other interests obtained legislation to amend the "economic laws."

The tariff question further illustrated the division of interest between the larger and the smaller mining companies. The latter supported an attempt by Pittman to include a duty of thirty cents per ounce in the Hawley-Smoot Act of 1930. They undoubtedly agreed that, as the senator told a colleague, "our silver mines in Nevada are in deplorable condition." While the benefits of such a duty would be of substantial help to miners in the West, he expected opposition from "the Guggenheim interests and others . . . who only smelt and refine American silver and produce their own silver [elsewhere]."[32] (These companies had subsidiaries operating in Canada and Latin America, from which they imported metallic concentrates for processing.) The smelter operators argued, however, that such a duty would be futile since domestic production exceeded the nation's consumption.[33] Doubtless Pittman knew that American Smelting had retained Charles S. Thomas to present its objections to this tariff before the appropriate congressional committees. Later the senator specifically acknowledged to his former colleague the effectiveness of "Guggenheim" influences in defeating his proposal in the House of Representatives.[34]

In the twenties, Pittman echoed the demands of small producers. He fought to extend purchases by the Treasury under the Pittman Act; he advocated an export association and improved credit facilities for companies with limited capital; he sponsored an import duty on silver. His pleas were ineffective, however, and he could only complain about the situation. "The fact that we cannot compete with the cheap [imported] silver is demonstrated," he said, "by the steady fall in the price, the closing down of our mines and the decreasing production in the United States."[35] He did not acknowledge that the mines also closed because of depletion, low-grade ores, and unprofitable prices for the base metals.[36]

Pittman seemed to forget that domestic production exceeded consumption and that the silver industry needed to expand foreign demand. The greatest opportunities for foreign expansion were in the Far East, an area where silver was highly valued as well as being the primary circulating medium. Observers assumed that the hoards of bullion in China and India were very large since it was known that these two nations absorbed approximately 70 percent of the world supply after 1920.[37]

Throughout the twenties, executives in the silver industry had been constantly watchful of economic developments in the Far East. China's increasing consumption during the decade, and particularly in 1927 and 1928 when its absorption of silver exceeded all previous records, no doubt pleased Brownell and his associates at American Smelting. But that rise only temporarily offset the effect of a monetary change initiated by the government of India. The Royal Commission of Indian Currency and Finance had released a report in London in August of 1926 recommending that a substantial portion of the government of India's stock of monetary silver be sold in order to purchase gold. The mere publication of that recommendation precipitated a sharp break in prices for silver, but they stabilized thereafter at approximately fifty-five cents per ounce. Many feared that India's entire supply, which exceeded three years of world production, might be dumped on the market. By 1930 it had sold over a hundred

11

million ounces, causing American producers increasing concern over the future direction of Indian silver policy.[38]

While in London in August of 1930, Brownell talked with officials about discontinuing India's sales of demonetized silver. By then, prices had been slowly declining for more than nine months. He evidently hoped that worsening economic conditions and diminishing return would produce a policy reversal at the India Office, but he was disappointed. Brownell learned that sales would continue in order to purchase the gold needed to maintain India's monetary standard, and that its duty of four cents per ounce on imported silver would be retained indefinitely. Officials there assured him, however, that no plan existed to dispose of the entire stock of silver. Moreover, sales had been made in small lots, a practice which would continue in order to limit disruption of the world market.[39]

After returning to New York, Brownell sought support from the Hoover administration for a plan he had devised to stabilize the world silver market. He urged negotiation of marketing agreements by governments most concerned with the white metal. The major producing nations were Mexico, the United States, Canada, and Peru; those inclined toward reducing their stocks were India, China, France, and Spain. Through William Loeb, also an executive at American Smelting, Brownell's proposal came to the attention of two of Loeb's friends in Washington: Acting Secretary of the Treasury Ogden L. Mills and President Herbert Hoover. The latter told Mills that Brownell's plan "impresses me rather seriously and I would be glad to have your views as to anything we can do in the matter."[40] Apparently, Mills adopted a less favorable view since the Treasury failed to initiate relevant action.

Inaction by the federal government led Brownell to seek support from the Silver Bloc. Employing indirect means to broach the subject with William E. Borah of Idaho, chairman of the Senate Committee on Foreign Relations, Brownell wrote to Irvin E. Rockwell, the senator's old friend, constituent, and a mining man. In turn, Rockwell quoted excerpts from Brownell's letter in one of his own to "Dear Billie." Carefully preparing the way,

Rockwell reported that "Brownell is an old Idaho man, formerly a practicing attorney, and one of the strong men we have sent East." He then outlined Brownell's plan and quoted his comment that:

> In my judgment there is no possibility of doing anything for silver so long as India remains a seller. Other countries . . . should also abstain. [If these] nations would agree not to sell their silver, a temporary makeshift arrangement might be made without the necessity of International Conference or new legislation.

Rockwell endorsed Brownell's ideas and commended the executive's opposition to sales or loans of silver by any government, noting that the price of silver was then only thirty-three cents per ounce. "I wish you could meet Mr. Brownell," Rockwell commented.[41]

Early in 1931, Brownell expanded his drive for political action by seeking help from his western business associates and friends, including Charles S. Thomas. "It would greatly support the efforts being made to have the administration take action toward stabilizing silver," Brownell wrote to each of them, "if it were requested to do so by each State Legislature." He provided an informational pamphlet and suggested that "each resolution had best be prepared locally, as it would thus be more apt to present the local viewpoint." Brownell added, however, that the resolutions should

> refer to the drastic fall in silver, its effects upon our Oriental trade, particularly China, its connection with the present world industrial crisis, and the possibility of stabilizing the value of silver by international cooperation, formal or informal, and ask that steps be taken to accomplish this result.[42]

Brownell's western associates readily won the votes of state legislators. As to their individual attitudes, perhaps that of Charles S. Thomas was typical. He said: "I need hardly give you the assurance that I will to the best of my ability promote the acceptance of your views in every possible way."[43]

Support from the West may have materially hastened the Senate's action. That body approved without dissent a proposal introduced by Key Pittman after acceptance by Borah's Foreign Relations Committee.[44] Senate Resolution 442 not only authorized the president to call an international silver conference, it also approved American participation in negotiations leading to suspension of sales.[45]

Brownell viewed the Senate's resolution as only an initial action in a movement that should proceed cautiously. He counseled Charles S. Thomas to be patient since the conference should not be held "until economic thought has been able to crystallize on the subject to some greater extent." Brownell also argued that:

An international conference should be, so far as possible, called under the auspices of both England and the United States and to have it associated in the public mind with the distress of the silver miner would be very unfortunate. . . . In short, a movement in which silver miners are so prominent as to give the impression that the movement is in the interest of the mining industry would receive about as much public support as would a convention of livery stable keepers asking action to restrict the automobile and restore their vanished business.[46]

More than a year elapsed before Herbert Hoover decided to participate in an international conference on economic problems. During the intervening months unemployment increased, commerce and trade declined, and many nations abandoned the gold standard. The impact of these events, the demands by silverites, and the approach of national elections finally prompted the president to accept a British invitation to a conclave. Meanwhile, newspaper and magazine comments on the Senate resolution left no doubt that financial interests were opposed to a conference devoted exclusively to the subject of silver.

During 1931, articles criticizing the reviving silver movement appeared in national publications. The authors objected to the Senate's calling for an international conference and to arguments justifying such a gathering. These writers seemed impelled to refute the silver agitation. Ranging from mild to intense opposition, titles included: "The Silver Problem," "Silver and the Business Depression," "Silver—Some Fundamentals," "The Unimportance of Silver," and "Silver—A Senate Racket." Generally, the authors disavowed the silverites' goals as well as their tactics.

Of the six representative articles, the one entitled "The Silver Problem" contained the most thoughtful analysis. Its author, Herbert B. Ellison, forcefully noted:

> The nations are beginning to dispense with gold as well as silver. . . . So far have we progressed from the days when we insisted on "honest metal" as a safeguard against dishonest government that the movement to reinstate more silver into circulation seems foredoomed to failure.[47]

Ellison correctly assessed the long-run trend for monetary gold and silver, but his prediction for their immediate future proved faulty. Also significant was his mention of distrust for government officials. Few writers noted that the bimetallists wanted to avoid both private and public mechanisms restricting the easy flow of money and credit; to them, "free silver" meant, somehow, free men.[48]

Four of the six writers dwelt upon the international economic crisis. Each asserted that legislation would achieve very little, and that only natural economic processes could improve the complex silver situation. In short, they said the low price of silver was a result of the world-wide depression and was of minor importance, at most, as a cause of that depression. These writers also insisted upon the irreversibility of the well-established trend toward its demonetization. Finally, only Ellison found merit in the idea of an international agreement to prevent selling by governments.[49]

Two articles concentrating on domestic politics and monetary agitation took vigorous exception to silverite designs to enhance the white metal's status. The authors were Joseph Stagg Lawrence, a well-known financial writer, and Neil Carothers, a college professor and economist. Both compared at length the declining importance of silver, despite its illustrious heritage,

15

with the demands of western silver interests for governmental aid to artificially restore the value of their product. Their articles were partisan diatribes written for popular appeal, and published in widely read magazines. Charles S. Thomas wrote a reply to Lawrence's article entitled, "The Unimportance of Silver."[50] When editors of *World's Work* refused to publish the rebuttal, however, Thomas reluctantly turned to the *Congressional Record*.[51]

In replying to Lawrence, Thomas stressed the bimetallists' basic ideals. He pointed out the movement's humanitarian goals, its call for political morality, and its intellectual honesty. Remonetization, he insisted, was the common people's only means to defeat the control by financial manipulators over gold and thus over all credit. Arguing that the monetary mismanagement which had caused the depression necessitated a legislated, bimetallic reform, he rejected opposition arguments based on the plethora of silver. Oversupply was the result of government action, he said, and it would be eliminated when governments remonetized silver.[52]

The editors of the *North American Review* courteously published Brownell's temperate, realistic answer to Professor Carothers' immoderate writings.[53] In "Silver—Its Future as Money," he acknowledged that Carothers stated "in an exaggerated and prejudiced form the opinion as to silver more or less vaguely held by many people." The executive claimed, however, that the professor had failed "to distinguish between the noise made by the silver interests and the real underlying causes of the various silver movements." Brownell then suggested that the fundamental problem was the growing shortage of monetary gold in an era of rapid economic expansion. His conclusion was that governments must adopt either silver or paper.[54]

Brownell was not alone in his perception of the basic problem underlying silverite agitation. Professor John R. Commons wrote Senator John J. Blaine of Wisconsin in 1931 in support of the demands for more money. Commons said: "I believe the present world-wide fall in commodity prices is not due to overproduction but to the scarcity of gold caused by bringing many nations to the gold standard, along with these sales of silver by governments in silver using countries." This eminent economist endorsed "bimetallism with free coinage at a fixed ratio, say 20 to 1." He added: "This money problem is more important, for the next several years, than all other economic problems combined."[55]

The fact that monetary specialists like Carothers heatedly disagreed with Commons' analysis encouraged the popular discussion of monetary beliefs. Congressman Edgar Howard of Nebraska, who once was a secretary for William Jennings Byran, demanded in 1931 a greater quantity of money in order to ease the depression.

It is now quite generally conceded that the volume of money in any country has much to do with the price of commodities and labor. If the volume be small, easily controlled by powerful financial interests, commodities cannot move freely, trade becomes stagnant and labor unemployed. If the volume be large enough to supply the legitimate needs of trade, then the exchange of commodities is unhampered, and the products of agriculture and the factory rise to a fair profit above the cost of production.[56]

A large number, perhaps a majority, of western and southern farmers subscribed to Congressman Howard's monetary notions. Numerous other persons, including Professor Commons, thought this approach possessed essential validity, if not technical accuracy.

The importance of the money question was political, not intellectual. Many persons were certain that declining trade and prices did not result from an excess of products on the market but from an inadequate supply of currency in actual circulation. At least one easterner, Franklin D. Roosevelt, governor of New York, comprehended the significance of this conviction. His later decisions on monetary policy were to align him with those who realized that beneath the surface of this incomplete explanation lay at least a valid grievance.[57]

By 1931, economic conditions in mining and agriculture brought forth agitation to "do something for silver." The western

17

senators responded quickly to these demands because they firmly believed that the federal government should intervene to restore prices and purchasing power. Their insistence upon prompt and effective action in Washington soon echoed in the halls of Congress and reverberated in the White House.

1. Claudius O. Johnson, *Borah of Idaho* (New York: Longmans, Green and Co., 1936), pp. 79, 223, 397–400, 444–445.
2. Burton K. Wheeler with Paul F. Healy, *Yankee from the West* (Garden City, New York: Doubleday and Company, Inc., 1962), pp. 104–64, 196, 213–15, 250–65, 400–15.
3. Fred L. Israel, *Nevada's Key Pittman* (Nebraska: University of Nebraska Press, 1963), *passim*.
4. *Ibid.*, pp. 32–33.
5. Milton R. Merrill, *Reed Smoot, Utah Politician* (Monograph Series, I, No. 2 [Logan, Utah: Utah State University Press, April, 1953]), 5–6; Thomas C. Donnelly (ed.), *Rocky Mountain Politics* (Albuquerque: University of New Mexico Press, 1940), p. 31; U.S., *Congressional Directory*, 73d Cong., 2d Sess. (January, 1934), pp. 117–18.
6. U.S., *Congressional Directory*, 73d Cong., 2d Sess. (January, 1934), pp. 5, 13.
7. The agricultural interests were represented by the Farm Bloc. It included senators and representatives from southern, western, and some middle western states. In the thirties, leadership of this Bloc fell to senators Ellison D. Smith of South Carolina, chairman of the Committee on Agriculture and Forestry, and Elmer Thomas of Oklahoma, the Senate's most outspoken advocate of monetary inflation. Burton K. Wheeler also was an influential member of this group. In the spring of 1933, they wielded thirty-six votes in matters pertinent to farm legislation and inflation. John L. Shover, *Cornbelt Rebellion: The Farmers' Holiday Association* (Urbana, Illinois: The University of Illinois Press, 1965), pp. 103–104.
8. Y. S. Leong, *Silver: An Analysis of the Factors Affecting Its Price* (Washington: The Brookings Institution, 1933), pp. 29, 60, 69, 81–84; Dickenson H. Leavens, *Silver Money* (Bloomington, Indiana: Principia Press, Inc., 1939), pp. 162, 354.
9. The number of producing mines fell from 3,300 in 1910 to 2,300 in 1920, and that trend continued. U.S., Geological Survey, *Mineral Resources of the United States: 1920*, Part 1, p. 531; U.S., Bureau of Mines, *Mineral Survey of the United States: 1930*, Part 1, p. 827.
10. U.S., *Statutes at Large*, XL, Part 1, Public Law No. 139, 535–37; Leavens, *Silver Money*, pp. 140–41, 145–50. See also Israel, pp. 75–78.
11. Leavens, *Silver Money*, pp. 160–61.
12. *Engineering and Mining Journal-Press*, CXIV (September 9, 1922), 471–72.
13. *Ibid.*
14. Leavens, *Silver Money*, pp. 148–49; U.S., *Congressional Record*, 67th Cong., 4th Sess., 1923, LXIV, Part 6 (March 3, 1923), 5263; *Engineering and Mining Journal-Press*, CXV (January-April, 1923), 201, 246, 335, 463, 772.

15. U.S., Congress, Senate, Commission of Gold and Silver Inquiry, *Progress Report of Senate Commission of Gold and Silver Inquiry*, 68th Cong., 1st Sess., 1924, pp. 21–45.

16. *Ibid.*, p. 17; *Engineering and Mining Journal-Press*, CXVI (September 15, 1923), 467–68.

17. *Engineering and Mining Journal-Press*, CXVI (September 15, 1923), 467–68.

18. *Ibid.*

19. *Ibid.* (December 1, 1923), 952. The committee had fifteen members including producers from Arizona, California, Colorado, Montana, Nevada, Utah, and three major companies headquartered in the East, Anaconda, American Smelting, and the United States Smelting, Refining and Mining Company.

20. It was formed under authority of the Webb-Pomerene Act of 1918 which specified conditions under which cooperative action by competitors directed toward the promotion of exports would not be subject to antitrust prosecution. It was barred from engaging in the domestic trade or acting to raise prices in that market. U.S., *Statutes at Large*, XL, 1918, Part I, Public Law No. 126, 516–18.

21. Henry N. Rives to Charles S. Thomas, January 25, 1927, Charles S. Thomas Papers (State Historical Society of Colorado Library, Denver, Colorado), Pittman silver case folder. Hereafter cited as Thomas Papers. *Engineering and Mining Journal-Press*, CXVIII (August 16, 1924), 265–66.

22. *Mines Register*, XIX (1937), 861–63. From 1924 to 1933, this company produced 22,433,363 ounces of silver, plus lead, copper, zinc, and gold. Its revenues for 1929 totaled $4,088,419.

23. Rives to Thomas, January 25, 1927, Thomas Papers, Pittman silver case folder.

24. Rives to Key Pittman, May 27, 1933, Key Pittman Papers (Manuscripts Division, Library of Congress, Washington, D.C.), box 145, "R" folder. Hereafter cited as Pittman Papers. Pittman told another correspondent that ". . . no other association in my opinion would be a success." Pittman to Roy Ridge, October 30, 1933.

25. Isaac F. Marcosson, *Metal Magic: The Story of the American Smelting and Refining Company* (New York: Farrar, Straus and Company, 1949), pp. 94–96, 104–06.

26. *Mines Register*, XIX (1937), 23, 31, 59, 728, 964.

27. Thomas to Rives, January 1, 1926, Thomas Papers, Pittman Bill, 1926, folder.

28. Brownell to Thomas, January 19, 1926, Thomas Papers. Ferry agreed with Brownell because farmers were "blissfully ignorant of the whole silver thing." Ferry to Brownell, January 15, 1926.

29. Brownell to Thomas, February 26, 1926, Thomas Papers.

30. U.S., *Progress . . . Inquiry*, pp. 12–17; Israel, pp. 80–81; Everett L. Cooley, "Silver Politics in the United States, 1918–1946" (unpublished Ph.D. dissertation, Department of History, University of California, 1951), pp. 38–43.

31. Thomas P. Lamont to Tasker L. Oddie, January 14, 1930, NCRE–509 (Records of the Department of Commerce, National Archives, Social and Economic Branch, Washington, D.C.), Silver, 1930, file. Hereafter cited as NCRE–509.

32. Pittman to William H. King, June 29, 1929, Pittman Papers, box 101, Silver tariff folder.

33. Charles S. Thomas, "Supplemental Brief of American Smelting and

Refining Company," James L. Geary to William Loeb, June 29, 1929, Thomas Papers, Correspondence and Scrapbooks, 1920–1929 folder.

34. Pittman to Thomas, April 30, 1930, Pittman Papers, box 101, Silver tariff folder; Israel, pp. 82–83.

35. Pittman to Alben Barkley, June 13, 1929, Pittman Papers, box 101, Silver tariff folder.

36. *Engineering and Mining Journal,* CXXIX (April 7, 1930), 331.

37. Leong, pp. 41, 52, 122–23.

38. Government of India, *Report of the Controller of the Currency . . . 1927, 1928, 1929,* as cited in Leavens *Silver Money,* pp. 175, 179, 181–82. After listening to remarks by Brownell at a producers' meeting, Charles S. Thomas told Pittman that "the silver industry . . . is threatened with virtual annihilation. . . ." Thomas to Pittman, September 23, 1926, Thomas Papers, Pittman Bill letters and contracts folder.

39. Francis H. Brownell to Julius S. Klein, September 16, 1930, NCRE–509, Silver, 1930, file.

40. William Loeb to Ogden Mills, October 28, 1930, and Herbert Hoover to Ogden Mills, November 10, 1930, NCRD–56 (Records of the Department of the Treasury, National Archives, Social and Economic Branch, Washington, D.C.), Silver Miscellaneous, 1921–1931, file.

41. Irvin E. Rockwell to William E. Borah, December 10, 1930, William E. Borah Collection (Washington State University Library, Pullman, Washington). Hereafter cited as Borah Collection. Rockwell aided Brownell on several subsequent occasions, and in 1934, American Smelting provided assistance for Rockwell's mining venture. Rockwell to Borah, June 1, 1934.

42. Brownell to Thomas, January 17, 1931, Thomas Papers, Thomas re silver folder.

43. Thomas to Brownell, January 20, 1931, Thomas Papers; Israel, p. 87.

44. Pittman introduced a second resolution (S.R. 443) at the same time but it was tabled. That resolution is discussed in Chapter 3.

45. U.S., *Congressional Record,* 71st Cong., 3d Sess., 1931, LXXIV, Part 6 (February 21, 1931), 4557.

46. Brownell to Thomas, September 25, 1930, Thomas Papers, Thomas re silver folder.

47. Herbert B. Ellison, "The Silver Problem," *Foreign Affairs,* IX (April, 1931), 452.

48. "Free silver" meant coinage of silver without a mintage charge—the sovereign power of seigniorage. In the nineteenth century this political slogan acquired connotative meaning indicating popular indignation over the demonetization of silver (called the "Crime of '73") and the repeal of the Sherman Silver Purchase Act's purchasing clause in 1893. In 1896, it also carried the meaning of "national bimetallism." Leavens, *Silver Money,* p. 58.

49. Ellison, "The Silver Problem," *Foreign Affairs,* IX (April, 1931), 441–56; Dickenson H. Leavens, "Silver and the Business Depression," *Harvard Business Review,* IX (April, 1931), 330–38; Herbert M. Bratter, "Silver—Some Fundamentals," *Journal of Political Economy,* XXXIX (June, 1931), 21–68; Frank D. Graham, "The Fall in the Value of Silver and Its Consequences," *Journal of Political Economy,* XXXIX (August, 1931), 425–70.

50. Joseph Stagg Lawrence, "The Unimportance of Silver," *World's Work,* LX (August, 1931), 21–25, 66–67.

51. Thomas to Russell Doubleday, October 5, 1931, and Thomas to Frank J. Cannon, October 28, 1931, Thomas Papers, Thomas re silver folder.

52. U.S., *Congressional Record*, 72d Cong., 1st Sess., 1931, LXXV, Part 1 (December 15, 1931), 514–17.

53. Neil Carothers, "Silver—A Senate Racket," *North American Review*, CCXXXIII (January, 1932), 4–15.

54. Francis H. Brownell, "Silver—Its Future as Money," *North American Review*, CCXXXIII (March, 1932), 234–42.

55. Commons to Blaine, May 15, 1931, Pittman Papers, box 141, College folder.

56. *Denver Post*, November 15, 1931.

57. One of these was Irving Fisher, a professor of political economy at Yale University, who said that it was "not too much goods but rather too little money that explains . . . [falling prices]." Irving Fisher, "Reflation and Deflation," *Annals of the American Academy of Political and Social Science*, CLXXI (January, 1934), 129. Fisher also held that "the depression, beginning with the stock market crash, was very largely due to the insufficiency of the metallic base."

2 The Silver Bloc

DURING 1931 two major themes developed within the silver movement: the first centered about finding markets for the white metal; the second revealed rivalry among members of the Senate Silver Bloc. Of the proposals to aid the industry, only the efforts to convene an international conference made significant headway. By the following spring, the Hoover administration agreed to participate in a monetary and economic conference to be held in London.

Rivalry among the silver senators often impeded progress for the silver cause. Conflicting personalities, aspirations, and political circumstances caused incessant wrangling. They argued over goals, tactics, and leadership. Although these clashes occasionally became intense, they were encounters between men who shared fundamental faith in the economic and monetary importance of silver.

However, these senators, after a great deal of struggle among themselves, derived at least some degree of cohesion from common motivation. They desired not only reelection, but aid for an industry long important in the West. Each was associated with mining in some way and most no doubt invested in the mines. Certainly the senators knew many persons engaged in that business and others dependent upon its prosperity. The combined talents of these able politicians made them formidable. Individually and in concert, they urged the president to actions favorable to producers. Herbert Hoover acquiesced to their demands during his last year in office, although earlier he had seemed unimpressed with silverite pleas.

In the spring of 1931, Utah's Senator King temporarily became the spokesman for those urging the president to call an international conference on silver. Responding to requests by constituents, King attended an International Chamber of Commerce convention meeting at Washington. He asked that organization to endorse the Senate's resolution requesting the president to initiate plans for an international conference. Also, he presided at a luncheon for delegates interested in such a conference from Denmark, France, Canada, Japan, China, India, and the United States. Although not an official delegate, he was named chairman of a special committee to discuss the problem.[1]

King's efforts led the International Chamber of Commerce to approve a resolution mildly favoring a conference. He later told Charles S. Thomas that his committee "discussed the question quite fully and agreed that we would get behind the resolution offered by Mr. Pei, one of the Chinese delegates, and make it stronger if possible."[2] King conceded to Thomas that there was "strong opposition to any mention of the silver question." The senator also mentioned his embarrassment at not being a delegate, an omission which had prevented his taking the issue to the convention floor. Still, King was pleased because the resolution would "compel discussion in many countries of the silver question and its relation to economic conditions."[3]

The senator from Utah continued to press the matter. He told Charles Thomas that he had been "rather insistent upon a committee being appointed to carry out the purpose of the resolution."[4] Such a committee—composed of businessmen interested in the matter, plus Senators King and Pittman—was formed to act unofficially. Its objective accorded with the resolution, which asked the delegates to request their respective governments to consider the calling of an international conference to discuss the silver problem.[5] A few weeks later, Reed Smoot undercut his colleague from Utah while speaking to a group of mining men in Salt Lake City. With King seated nearby, he unexpectedly read a telegram from Herbert Hoover which said that informal discussion had revealed that several important nations were opposed to such proceedings at that time.[6]

Indignant over Hoover's support of Smoot's tactics, King hurriedly returned to Washington and found an opportunity to retaliate. During a press conference, he castigated the president for doing too little to fight the depression and for his continued faith in monometallism. "The demand for gold is a selfish demand," King averred; "it takes cognizance only of the creditor class."[7] The irate senator later learned that his colleagues objected to this rash outburst against Hoover. In a sharply-worded letter, Pittman, for example, pointed out to King that the strong assertions he had made before the monometallists were a mistake because their cooperation was essential. Pittman said that while he, too, was a bimetallist, he would never admit it publicly.[8] Other evidence indicates that Senator Borah also disavowed King's remarks.[9]

The senator from Utah seemed frustrated. "I do not know whether we are making any progress in bringing about an international conference," he told Charles S. Thomas. King described all of his efforts on behalf of the metal during the preceding two months, and conceded to his former colleague that the movement had little prospect in the future. "We have no organization and few who are deeply interested in the matter."[10] The Senator needed a vacation.

In a more restrained manner than that of King, Senator Borah revealed his growing concern over monetary problems and the possible role of silver in their solution. He took this stance easily. The "Lion of Idaho" had been a Silver Republican in 1896 and he had not lost his populistic suspicion of the "money power," as he proved in a radio address delivered in May, 1931. After his talk, Charles Thomas wrote that he was pleased to hear Borah's voice "again lifted in behalf of the bimetallic system of currency." Continuing, he expressed his doubts over prospects for "the proposed conference." The selection of delegates was vitally important, Thomas insisted, for "if this movement miscarries, it is the end of silver as money."[11]

Borah and Thomas agreed to present the silver problem as a world economic question. Senator Borah emphasized in a letter to Thomas that the movement should not be regarded as one mainly of benefit to the mining industry. He also believed that

25

there was need to arouse interest in the matter throughout the country "to compel attention upon the part of those who stand in places of authority."[12]

While Borah acknowledged the need for action, he avoided personal involvement. Admitting that he was becoming "a little out of patience," Borah, nevertheless, rejected Senator King's suggestion that they personally initiate a campaign. He preferred that the matter be taken up by men in the business world who possessed "the means and the willingness to do the work."[13]

On July 27, 1931, Borah met with Smoot at Boise to decide upon a workable strategy. Conferring with them were a group of producers from Salt Lake City, and Borah's close friend Irvin E. Rockwell. Letters written afterward by participants outlined the agreement made by these silver advocates. They decided unanimously to attempt to secure an international monetary conference. Phrased another way, they agreed to work for "rehabilitation of silver as a basic money metal . . . [by obtaining international cooperation to that end]."[14]

Borah told Smoot that he opposed "any scheme which . . . regard[s] silver as a commodity and undertakes to peg [its] price. . . ." He sought the white metal's equality with gold as a basis for credit, and for the issue of paper money. He objected in principle to treating it as a mere commodity because that would only retard solution of the silver question. Despite his personal preferences, Borah said he would not stand in the way of Smoot's sponsoring a plan to accept the metal at a fixed price from foreign governments in payment of their war debts.[15]

Several other western senators also endorsed Borah's advocacy of an international monetary conference. In the weeks following, King, Pittman, and Edward P. Costigan of Colorado said they agreed with his proposal. As explained by Rockwell to a mine official at Kellogg, Idaho, Borah proposed to guide the movement down "the middle of the trail," avoiding both "go-it-alone" bimetallism and any plan treating silver as primarily a commodity.[16] Later that year, however, the various silver advocates continued to contradictorily urge (1) increasing prices, (2) a fixed price, or (3) restoration of the metal to a ratio of value with gold.

An unusually somber and doubtful mood dominated the capital city when the silver senators returned in the fall of 1931. The country seemed to be moving toward a financial crisis. Abandonment of the gold standard by Great Britain and twelve other sterling bloc nations in September had occasioned a serious drain on the American supply of gold. Moreover, the continuing deflation of property values had created a feeling of urgency throughout the country.

The accumulating load of serious troubles pervading the atmosphere of Washington encouraged a widening discussion of the silver issue. Upon returning to the East, Senator Borah testified to a resurging interest in the money question which he had discovered in the interior states. In a letter to Irvin Rockwell he said:

I spoke at Sioux City, Iowa, on my way to Washington, and I was amazed at the interest manifested in that part of the country on the subject. I feel there ought to be as much discussion of the subject as is practicable in the Middle West.[17]

With the silver question being discussed once again, it was fitting that the octogenarian author of *Coin's Financial School,* William H. "Coin" Harvey, led a mass meeting at which he demanded reform because "the present monetary system is a monster."[18] Growing public acceptance of such discussion prompted Borah to advise openly that an international conference would improve economic conditions by establishing a ratio of value between gold and silver.[19]

Senator Pittman also noted the increasing talk about silver and monetary problems. He echoed Borah's call for an international conference both to newspaper reporters and to an eastern radio audience. However, Pittman insisted that he only sought an "international conference to fix the price of silver."[20] At that time, he believed it was best to allow "the market to seek the natural level rather than to attempt to artificially stabilize silver at fifty cents an ounce."[21] Favorable public reaction raised the senator's hopes, apparently, and he rejected a set support price for the white metal.

27

In a manner reminiscent of bygone times, staple commodity growers renewed their interest in silver. Both tobacco and cotton men were disposed toward cooperation because the low exchange rate of silver had reduced the ability of China, an important foreign market, to import their commodities. A spokesman reported to Pittman that, according to the tobacco industry's annual reports, export sales had declined by 3,500,000 cigarettes, a reduction "accounted for entirely by the decrease in exports to China." Therefore, he wrote, "the tobacco people would be happy to join forces with the silver interests to stabilize the price of silver."[22]

Cotton men had equal reason to support the silver movement. In an article published in the *New York Times,* Pittman asserted that in 1930 British sales of cheap cotton goods to China had declined by 70 percent. That nation's imports would not return to normal, the senator warned, while its purchasing power was reduced by the low exchange rate for its silver money.[23] Pittman put forward this theme in the Senate as well, and with a political twist. He complained that the Hoover administration had said nothing and done nothing about the silver problem while the exporters of cotton and tobacco and other products continued to suffer.[24]

In spite of the improving circumstances and support from willing allies, silver men continued to ventilate their differences. Those who failed to see virtue in a middle course included western senators, silver producers, and monetary reformers. Generally, advocates of price-pegging favored the gold standard first and foremost, and thereafter sought a gradually rising price for silver. The bimetallists, on the other hand, asserted that the gold standard was at least in need of assistance. This could best be provided by granting to silver full equality with gold at a ratio of value fixed independently by the United States.

The conflicting attitudes frustrated Key Pittman. "Our silver crowd here have lost their nerve," he complained; "I have not been able to get any help whatever from any of them."[25] He telegraphed W. Mont. Ferry that December, asking him to start a publicity campaign to develop greater public understanding of the silver question. Pittman told him that the recent European monetary changes made such a campaign imperative, but "our [Senate] committee cannot engage in this work."[26]

The silver producers' hesitation was easily explained. Solomon R. Guggenheim, a member of the wealthy New York firm which controlled American Smelting and other mining enterprises, preached caution. In a newspaper interview, Guggenheim said he opposed the calling of a "premature international conference" on silver. He also said that while a gradual rise in the price of silver was not undesirable, the most recent rise troubled him because it was due to speculation. This type of increase was unfortunate, he believed, since price stability, not fluctuation, was needed to promote trade with the Orient.[27] Guggenheim's opinion matched that of Senator Oddie. While speaking early that December to delegates at the American Mining Congress in Philadelphia, Oddie made no mention of the call for an international conference and he specifically rejected bimetallism. He favored a gradual restoration of all metal prices to their levels prior to World War I.[28]

The major producers supported an alternative conference plan which Senator Pittman immediately tried to discredit. To his chagrin, the American Mining Congress adopted a resolution calling upon the government of India and the major silver producing countries—Canada, Mexico, Peru, and the United States —to negotiate an agreement limiting world market silver supplies. In a published telegram addressed to W. Mont. Ferry, Pittman charged that such an agreement would only hinder efforts to promote general intergovernmental accords. The senator labeled the new plan as "impossible of accomplishment" and merely "a subterfuge." Pittman placed the onus of this plan upon "the Guggenheims" and Republican Tasker L. Oddie, rather than upon the American Mining Congress.[29]

Silver senators from both parties worked at cross purposes. In December, 1931, Smoot introduced a bill (S. 1560) authorizing the payment of war debts in silver at a fixed price per ounce. Democrats Pittman, King, and Governor George H. Dern of Utah opposed the proposal. Dern telegraphed Smoot saying, "[It] is imperative that partisanship on [the] silver question be entirely eliminated as it is fundamentally economic in its nature."[30] Not surprisingly, Republicans, including Smoot, accused Democrats Pittman, King, and Dern of opposition for equally partisan reasons. Pittman answered, "I hear nothing of politics except from Utah."[31] These accusations did not disturb Borah, he told a perturbed constituent, because "Smoot's bill has only Smoot's vote."[32] However, Burton K. Wheeler submitted a bimetallism bill which could not be easily brushed aside.

Many silverites objected to agitation for bimetallism. Excepting Wheeler, the active silver senators—Democrats Pittman, King, and Costigan; Republicans Borah, Oddie, and Smoot—rejected the demands for independent bimetallism.[33] They viewed it as a serious threat to the silver cause and they feared its potential effect upon national politics; the issue might become a potent force in the West and the South, just as it had in the nineties when remonetization had split the major political parties along sectional lines. The Democrats worried most about this since the issue had served to perpetuate their party's minority status.

Wheeler chose to disregard the history of this issue. Early in January, the senator introduced Senate Bill 2487 to establish a bimetallic system of currency, to fix the relative value of gold and silver, and to provide for the free coinage of silver as well as gold.[34] In his remarks to the Senate later that month, Wheeler used traditional themes to justify the need for a major reform in the monetary system. He simply restated with recent illustrations the arguments of the nineties.

Wheeler told his colleagues that the remonetization would correct injustices to cotton, wheat, and laboring men which had developed in recent years due to the maloperation of the gold standard. He explained that gold had increased in value and reduced, for instance, the price of wheat from Russia and India on the world markets, thereby further depressing the prices received by American farmers for their wheat. Remonetization would increase the money supply and reduce the value of gold. Thereafter, prices would return to previous levels, he asserted, and farmers would be able to pay back their debts with dollars more nearly equal in value to those that were borrowed prior to

1929.[35] In sum, Senator Wheeler expressed the belief that re-monetizing silver would resuscitate the faltering economic machinery.

Eastern reaction to the bimetallism measure was harsh and ill founded. Newspaper editorialists, using the *New York Times* as a moderate example, commented alarmedly on the hoax called "free silver," the "irresponsible" actions of the western senators, and the "selfish" machinations of the silver producers.[36] The editorialists lacked factual information. Moreover, they rarely noted that Senator Wheeler's action represented the aspirations of many Montana voters. There were 11,842 miners in the state in 1930, or approximately 5 percent of the labor force; the 79,518 wheat farmers represented 37 percent of the labor force.[37]

Wheeler's bimetallism appealed to both of his state's major economic groups but not to officials of the Anaconda Company. Silver mining in Montana was almost entirely a by-product of that firm's copper mining operations. While its officers desired higher prices for silver, they did not seek independent bimetallism. Its president promptly endorsed another measure introduced a month later to draw away support from Wheeler's proposal.[38]

The Wheeler bill provided Republicans a seemingly perfect occasion to ridicule the Democrats. Apparently, they failed to do so out of respect for political cross currents. Republican leaders made no public statements about this bill, and when Wheeler discussed the reasons for its passage in the Senate, there were no rebuttals.[39] It is evident that Republicans were worried about the rural vote. The monetary crisis had spread throughout the nation and had sharply deflated western credits. The Hoover administration could only lose ground if the Wheeler bill precipitated a partisan debate on the money question.

Conflicting proposals led to talk of compromise. Additional silver bills were introduced in the Senate by Clarence C. Dill of Washington, John H. Bankhead of Alabama, and Borah. The cumulative effect dismayed previously hopeful observers. "The silver men in the West are very much disappointed," one executive from Spokane told Dill. "The ideas expressed in these bills are so conflicting that it is impossible for the friends of silver to get together on a concerted program."[40] Dill struggled to correct this situation: "I have been talking with Senators Pittman, Smoot, King and Wheeler and we have decided to have a conference of Western Senators . . . [to] see if we cannot agree on a united course of action."[41]

Spurred by election-year considerations, the Silver Bloc began to display cohesion. On January 28, 1932, its members met in the office of Senator Pittman "to discuss the advisability of forming an informal committee. . . ."[42] While their discussion was not recorded, the general result may be inferred from the senator's subsequent comment that they would submit Wheeler's bill first, and if it were rejected "then another and another" would be offered. He also said that they were considering a bill for "the purchase of American silver with silver certificates."[43]

Two weeks after the Silver Bloc's meeting, Pittman introduced a measure for the purchase of silver. Referred to the Banking and Currency Committee, it (S. 3606) authorized and directed the purchase of American-produced silver in limited amounts at the current market price with silver certificates.[44] Pittman lacked enthusiasm for this bill, he said, because it was "not what we desire but what we can obtain from Congress."[45] If enacted, it would provide a market for silver newly mined in the United States. The effect on world prices would be minor because American silver constituted only one-fifth of world production. The senator recognized this fact and expressed the hope that other governments might adopt similar legislation. He felt that if Canada, Mexico, and Peru took concerted action along with the United States, excesses would be absorbed eventually, permitting a return to normal market conditions.[46]

The American Silver Producers' Association shared Senator Pittman's dissatisfaction with the silver purchase bill, but for opposite reasons. Pittman learned that although the association's executive committee endorsed the bill, Brownell believed that certain restrictions were necessary because a sharp rise in prices might cause problems in the financing of trade with the Orient. The senator objected: "I rather regret that you consider it necessary to suggest to your banker friends such stringent limitations upon the operation of the act."[47] He acknowledged, however, that cooperation from Wall Street was vital both to finance the mining industry and to extract a favorable report on the measure from the Senate Committee on Banking and Currency.[48]

The silver purchase bill made minimal progress. Pressure by Smoot, Borah, and Pittman eventually resulted in a bare majority approval by the committee. It went no further, to Borah's disappointment. "We could put through the Pittman bill if it were not for the opposition . . . of the [Hoover] Administration," he commented.[49] Opposition strength was sufficient to discourage Pittman from presenting it to the Senate because, as he explained to a mining executive, "some say no vote is better than an adverse vote."[50]

Efforts to promote silver purchase legislation seemed a waste of time to bimetallists. They believed that the bloc lacked aggressiveness. One of them complained to Pittman that the "energy spent on silver purchase might better be spent winning some plan for the use of silver as a basic money."[51] Inflationists were more biting in their comments. The president of the National Farmers' Union, John A. Simpson, deplored the Pittman bill because it did not go far enough. He was "as strong for the remonetization of silver in 1932 as . . . in 1896."[52]

Despite the bimetallists' desire for action, the Wheeler bill did not come to a vote. It remained in Smoot's Committee on Finance throughout the session. Wheeler brought this matter to the attention of the Senate, deploring the fate of his measure; he directed his comments toward the senior senator from Utah, who, coincidentally, was up for reelection that fall.[53]

Although the silver senators made little legislative progress, events elsewhere tended to promote their cause. The world depression was steadily disrupting international trade. War debts and reparations payments were a burden to national treasuries and a source of international tension. In the United States, the pace of business continued to decline. Unemployment and hunger became prevalent as private sources of relief were exhausted. In short, economic crises at home and abroad justified the silver senators' demands for legislative action to halt the downward spiral.

The silver senators encountered formidable obstacles on the path toward an international conference. The outlook for such a conclave in the near future had not been encouraging in the spring of 1931, but one observer expressed optimism for its future prospects. Francis H. Brownell had learned on good authority, he told Charles S. Thomas, that "the Englishmen were willing to join in a conference, provided [it] was composed largely of experts and not of politicians." He believed that the matter was progressing "perhaps as effectively as can be expected under all the adverse circumstances . . . ,"[54] including opposition from the Hoover administration and several European governments. Added difficulties arose in Asia resulting from Mahatma Gandhi's passive resistance campaign in India and the instability of the national government of China due to the rebellion being led by Mao Tse-tung.

Desiring swift compliance with his demands for an international conference, Pittman had traveled in the Far East from May through July of that year. In China, he had conferred with financial and governmental leaders about organizing a conference. He believed that even though weak, its government at Nanking could initiate the proposal.[55] Pittman had refused to await an American initiative because, he said, "it appears that the President is afraid to make any move in this or any other matter."[56]

Pittman's visit to China was of questionable importance since he failed to gain immediate results, and claimed no achievements upon his return that August. His biographer has insisted that the senator's time was occupied by "social engagements and conversations with American merchants."[57] That assessment failed both to anticipate his later achievement at the London Economic Conference and to indicate the strength of his personal relationship with China's Minister of Finance, T. V. Soong. The senator's interest in China was indeed exceptional. The trip probably resulted in a delayed, yet positive, outcome for the silver cause.

During 1931 the senators had frequently asked the president

34

to initiate an international conference. They renewed their insistence after the sterling-bloc nations abandoned the gold standard that September. Borah discussed world conditions with Hoover early in October and suggested calling an international monetary conference.[58] The following day Pittman echoed this suggestion at a news conference and injected a political note:

If this question is not out of the way by next year, it is sure to be an issue in the campaign. I would regret its being made a partisan issue. . . . I hope the President will act before Congress meets and thereby take the issue out of politics.[59]

The two leading silver senators expressed contrasting views of the president's inaction. Borah confessed that his disappointment was keen, especially since Great Britain approved the idea.

I am satisfied that if there was a real, genuine move upon the part of our government for an international conference, we would get one. I am assured of that upon high authority in Great Britain. In fact, under present conditions they could not well refuse to take part in a program we would further and sincerely urge.[60]

Borah's disappointment later gave way to discontent. He conceded to Rockwell his distress over the president's continued reluctance to participate in any form of international discussions relative to silver.[61] Meanwhile, growing tolerance permeated the words of Key Pittman. The Nevadan readily conceded that "Japan's war in China [the Manchurian affair] has interferred materially with any accomplishments through international agreement. . . ."[62] Perhaps he believed this situation aided the Democrats.

Senator Pittman's tolerance for Hoover's inaction did not mean that he had reversed his own course. On the contrary, he continued to pursue his international conference goal, but with new tactics. In March, 1932, he solicited assistance from a British parliamentarian, Winston S. Churchill, who was then in New York City visiting their mutual friend, Bernard Baruch. Churchill had lost his post as chancellor of the Exchequer in 1929, but

35

he continued to be an influential politician. Furthermore, he had expressed to reporters his personal approval of proposals for an international silver conference.[63]

Pittman presented his ideas to Churchill through a letter transmitted by Baruch. The senator told the Briton of the impasse with Hoover in the initiation of the conference. However, the senator assured Churchill that Hoover would send delegates to any conference called by Great Britain.[64] Churchill's reaction to the letter was not recorded, but circumstantial evidence indicated that he soon transmitted its message to the chancellor of the Exchequer, Sir Neville Chamberlain.

In May of 1932, Churchill encouraged the British government to open international conference discussions with the Hoover administration. On May 10 in the House of Commons, Churchill questioned the British foreign secretary, Sir John Simon, after the latter had gratuitously mentioned that the chancellor of the Exchequer would "cooperate with others of good will" toward arranging an international conference on monetary matters. "Would [you] see," Churchill asked the secretary, "that that statement—that important statement—which he has made, is made known officially to the United States Government?" "It is not for me to bring it officially to the notice of any great and friendly Government . . . ," the foreign secretary replied, "but I do hope that they find it possible to read these Debates and to cast their eyes over any declarations which are made on behalf of the Government."[65] The content of Churchill's question and the secretary's response quickly reached the American embassy, if indeed its staff had not been unofficially forewarned. The embassy immediately sent word of "the Foreign Secretary's reply to Winston Churchill's question" to the acquiescent secretary of state, Henry L. Stimson, in Washington.[66]

The agreement to convene a conference came approximately two months after Pittman's communication to Churchill. On May 13, 1932, the British government asked the United States government to "consider whether the time had not come for the convocation of an international monetary and economic conference."[67] Hoover promptly acceded because he believed that the announcement of this conference would "contribute to a revival of hope."[68] To foster this attitude in the West, Hoover stipulated that the agenda include a discussion of silver.

The senators were suspicious of Hoover's reversal of attitude. Most observers viewed it as merely a grudging concession to silverite demands, and perhaps an attempt to outmaneuver the senators. The Republican leadership recently had blocked Senator King's resolution urging American participation in an international silver conference.[69] Mistrust came into the open when Hoover requested $40,000 to send a delegation to an "economic conference." Led by Borah, who claimed that "no one knows what an 'economic conference' means," the Senate changed the president's request to "monetary conference, including silver, to be held during 1932."[70]

Silverite reactions to the prospective conference were characteristically mixed. The initial response was favorable, especially as it presented evidence of accomplishment for the silver movement. Pittman expressed optimism that the silver problem would soon be solved, but he later had second thoughts about such a gathering. "Europe is so much more deeply interested in reparations and abolition of war debts," he told a silver producer, "that silver will be forgotten . . . [or] ignored."[71] Later, Pittman personally made certain that the white metal received the attention he believed it deserved from that international forum.

The silver cause had advanced several steps. After a decade of increasing difficulties for the producers, culminating in the plummeting prices of 1930, the Senate had adopted a resolution calling for an international conference. After another year of continued economic descent, the president had finally agreed to participate in an international consultation on problems relevant to the collapse of trade and monetary systems. Silver would be on the agenda, but its fate thereafter would depend upon the attitudes and exertions of the delegates.

1. *New York Times,* May 8, 1931.
2. King to Thomas, May 14, 1931, Thomas Papers, Thomas re silver folder.

3. *Ibid.* 4. *Ibid.*

5. *Ibid.* The *New York Times,* May 8, 1931, reported the presence of mining men from Utah at the committee meeting but they were not named. The report emphasized the strong differences between the delegates from Great Britain and those from India on the silver issue. It also mentioned that the author of the resolution, Tsuyee Pei, was managing director of the Bank of China at Shanghai.

6. William H. King to George H. Dern, June 8, 1931, George H. Dern Papers (Utah State Governors File, Utah State Historical Society, Salt Lake City, Utah), box 47, Silver folder; Hereafter cited as Dern Papers; *New York Times,* June 4, 1931.

7. *New York Times,* June 14, 1931.

8. Pittman to King, August 18, 1931, Pittman Papers, box 141, China trip folder.

9. Irvin E. Rockwell to William E. Borah, August 18, 1931, William E. Borah Papers (Manuscripts Division, Library of Congress, Washington, D.C.), box 328, Silver folder. Hereafter cited as Borah Papers.

10. King to Thomas, June 29, 1931, Thomas Papers, Thomas re silver folder.

11. Thomas to Borah, May 15, 1931, Thomas Papers.

12. Borah to Thomas, November 28, 1930; Borah to Frank J. Cannon, May 20, 1931; both in Borah Papers, box 328, Silver folder.

13. Borah to James P. McCarthy, May 25, 1931; Borah to King, July 9, 1931; both in Borah Papers, box 328, Silver folder.

14. Rockwell to Brownell, December 21, 1931, Borah Papers, box 340, Rockwell, Irvin E., folder; Frank B. Cook to Eleasar del Valle, July 28, 1931, Frank J. Cannon Papers (State Historical Society of Colorado Library, Denver, Colorado), Senator del Valle folder. Hereafter cited as Cannon Papers.

15. Borah to Smoot, August 18, 1931, Borah Papers, box 328, Silver folder; Leavens, *Silver Money,* pp. 239–41.

16. Rockwell to Stanley A. Easton, August 18, 1931; Rockwell to Borah, August 18, 1931; Rockwell to Brownell, December 21, 1931; all in Borah Papers, box 340, Irvin E. Rockwell folder; Costigan to Borah, September 11, 1931; Pittman to Borah, August 18, 1931; both in Borah Papers, box 328, Silver folder.

17. Borah to Rockwell, October 5, 1931, Borah Papers, box 328, Silver folder.

18. *Boston Evening Transcript,* August 26, 1931. Harvey led a series of meetings at his home town, Mont Ne, Arkansas.

19. *New York Times,* October 3, 1931.

20. *New York Times,* October 8, 1931. The *Times* published Pittman's text verbatim.

21. Pittman to Rene Leon, October 10, 1931, Pittman Papers, box 144, "L" folder.

22. E. Q. Yates to Pittman, November 18, 1931, Pittman Papers, box 139, Silver (1930–1935) folder. Yates quoted his information from *Tobacco Industry Annual Review* (1931).

23. *New York Times,* December 6, 1931.

24. U.S., *Congressional Record,* 72d Cong., 1st Sess., 1931, LXXV, Part 1 (December 10, 1931), 292–94.

25. Pittman to Frank L. Hardin, October 23, 1931, Pittman Papers, box 143, "H" folder.

26. Pittman to Ferry, December 3, 1931, Pittman Papers, box 142, "F" folder.
27. *New York Times,* November 11, 1931.
28. *Ibid.,* December 5, 1931.
29. *New York Times,* December 6, 1931.
30. Dern to Smoot, December 12, 1931, Dern Papers, box 47, Silver Stabilization folder.
31. Pittman to George W. Snyder, December 15, 1931, Pittman Papers, box 145, "S" folder.
32. Borah to James P. McCarthy, December 16, 1931, Borah Papers, box 340, Silver folder; U.S., *Congressional Record,* 72d Cong., 1st Sess., 1931, LXXV, Part 1 (December 14, 1931), 445.
33. *New York Times,* September 21, 1933.
34. U.S., *Congressional Record,* 72d Cong., 1st Sess., 1932, LXXV, Part 2 (January 4, 1932), 1164.
35. U.S., *Congressional Record,* 72d Cong., 1st Sess., 1932, LXXV, Part 3 (January 25, 1932), 2613–19.
36. *New York Times,* January 10, 1932.
37. Leonard J. Arrington, *The Changing Economic Structure of the Mountain West, 1850–1950* (Monograph Series, Vol. X, No. 3 [Logan, Utah: Utah State University Press, June, 1963]), pp. 36–37.
38. Henry N. Rives to Pittman, March 19, 1932, Pittman Papers, box 145, "R" folder.
39. U.S., *Congressional Record,* 72d Cong., 1st Sess., 1932, LXXV, Part 3 (January 25, 1932), 2613–19.
40. Frank M. Smith to Dill, January 16, 1932, Pittman Papers, box 145, "S" folder.
41. Dill to Frank M. Smith, January 13, 1931, Pittman Papers, box 145, "S" folder.
42. Pittman to John Janney, January 28, 1932, Pittman Papers, box 143, "J" folder. Pittman did not list the senators he expected to attend. This letter was dictated before the meeting.
43. Pittman to Charles S. Thomas, February 2, 1932, Pittman Papers, box 145, "T" folder.
44. U.S., *Congressional Record,* 72d Cong., 1st Sess., 1932, LXXV, Part 4 (February 11, 1932), 3733.
45. Pittman to Robert E. Tally, February 11, 1932, Pittman Papers, box 145, "T" folder.
46. *Ibid.*
47. Pittman to Brownell, March 12, 1932, Pittman Papers, box 140, "B" folder. Pittman first quoted from Brownell's letter recently received, dated March 11.
48. Pittman to Brownell, March 18, 1932, Pittman Papers, box 140, "B" folder.
49. Borah to Irvin E. Rockwell, May 26, 1932, Borah Papers, box 340, Silver folder.
50. Pittman to Frank M. Smith, July 14, 1932, Pittman Papers, box 145, "S" folder.
51. Simpson to Pittman, July 5, 1932, Pittman Papers, box 145, "S" folder.
52. Frank B. Cook to Pittman, February 17, 1932, Pittman Papers, box 141, "C" folder.
53. U.S., *Congressional Record,* 72d Cong., 1st Sess., 1932, LXXV, Part 10 (May 26, 1932), 11269–270.

39

54. Brownell to Thomas, May 31, 1931, Thomas Papers, Thomas re silver folder.

55. Pittman to Frank M. Smith, March 10, 1931, Pittman Papers, box 145, "S" folder.

56. Key Pittman to Norman H. Davis, March 20, 1931, Norman H. Davis Papers (Manuscripts Division, Library of Congress, Washington, D.C.), Key Pittman folder.

57. Israel, p. 86.   58. *New York Times,* October 3, 1931.

59. *Ibid.,* October 4, 1931.

60. Borah to James P. McCarthy, December 23, 1931, Borah Papers, box 340, Silver folder.

61. Borah to Irvin E. Rockwell, May 26, 1932, Borah Papers, box 340, Silver folder.

62. Pittman to Charles S. Thomas, February 2, 1932, Pittman Papers, box 145, "T" folder.

63. *New York Times,* October 3, 1931.

64. Pittman to Churchill, March 10, 1932, Pittman Papers, box 141, "C" folder.

65. Great Britain, *5 Parliamentary Debates* (Commons), CCLXV (1932), 1851.

66. U.S., Department of State, *Foreign Relations of the United States: Diplomatic Papers, 1932,* I, 811.

67. *Ibid.,* pp. 808–809.

68. Herbert Hoover, *The Memoirs of Herbert Hoover,* III, *The Great Depression, 1929–1941* (New York: The Macmillan Company, 1952), 130.

69. U.S., *Congressional Record,* 72d Cong., 1st Sess., 1932, LXXV, Part 9 (May 9, 1932), 9821. See Senate Joint Resolution No. 137.

70. *Ibid.,* LXXV, Part 13 (June 29, 1932), 14242–250; *New York Times,* June 30, 1932.

71. Pittman to Frank M. Smith, August 15, 1932, Pittman Papers, box 145, "S" folder; Israel, p. 89.

3 Western Silver Producers and the Silver Question

WHILE the Silver Bloc agitated for an international conference on silver during the early thirties, producers in the West began two additional campaigns to secure governmental markets for the white metal. The first was an attempt to obtain a substantial loan of the metal to the national government of China at Nanking and the second was an effort to win adoption of bimetallism by the United States. Neither of these campaigns succeeded, but each illustrated noteworthy aspects of the silver movement during the great depression.

Frank J. Cannon, long a partisan of the white metal, provided leadership for both of the western drives to aid its producers. In 1896 he had been elected to the Senate from Utah as a Silver Republican. During his two-year term he served on a commission to study the silver question. Thereafter, he had been a journalist and lecturer. In 1927 he retired and became associated with the Continental Divide Development Company, which owned mines near Aspen and Idaho Springs, Colorado, and maintained an office in Denver.[1] Persons who considered his background and interests were not surprised when late in life he again became very interested in silver and the money question.

During 1929, Cannon revealed his renewed concern for the white metal when he devised a scheme to provide silver bullion to the Nationalist government of China. Specifically, he proposed that the Treasury Department loan several hundred million ounces of silver to China on a long-term basis at little or no

41

interest. Repayment of this loan would be in silver by weight to avoid the problem of its fluctuating value in terms of gold. Cannon further proposed that the Treasury replace the metal loaned to China from current domestic production.[2]

The former senator also offered a rationale for the silver loan to China. He believed that an abundant supply of the metal in its coffers would strengthen the Nationalists' position in that country. He explained that China was a silver standard nation and that its new government at Nanking had encountered financial difficulties. Moreover, it also had trouble maintaining order in the provinces and it faced the constant threat of insurrection led by communists. He did not call attention to the obvious advantages for the American mining industry.[3]

Soon after the former senator evolved his loan plan, he attempted without success to obtain the president's endorsement. He explained it briefly to Herbert Hoover on April 3 and presented him a one-page résumé for further study. Thereafter, Cannon received no intimation of presidential interest, but he remained hopeful for many months.[4]

While Cannon awaited some sign about the proposal from Hoover, he also explained its features to his friends in the mining industry. After several visits to Utah, he eventually won the interest of a small group of Salt Lake City businessmen. To promote the plan, they formed the International Silver Commission in March of 1930, and named Cannon its chairman.[5]

The former senator had long been friendly with two members of the new commission: W. Mont. Ferry and George W. Snyder. Cannon had been active in politics with the former more than two decades earlier.[6] Snyder was related to Cannon and was involved in the affairs of the Continental Divide Development Company. He also owned mining properties in Utah, Idaho, and Nevada jointly with other members of his family plus an interest in the Combined Metals Reduction Company at Pioche, Nevada, a subsidiary of the National Lead Company.[7]

The International Silver Commission provided Cannon with funds for travel and for lobbying in Washington. Ferry, as president of the American Silver Producers' Association, assured his old friend that its executive committee in New York would authorize the necessary sums, promising $5,000 as a start. Promptly, Francis H. Brownell invited Cannon to present his plan to the members of the committee. They overruled Ferry, however, because the certainty of strong opposition to such a scheme made the effort unworthwhile.[8]

The commission ultimately obtained $27,000 to pay Cannon's expenses. It received $11,500 from Snyder, $3,000 from a mining associate of Ferry, and $7,500 from James Ellwood Jones, a West Virginia coal mine operator. Jones was associated with Snyder interests in a mining venture and was a friend of Gray Silver, an experienced lobbyist for farm organizations who assisted Cannon in Washington.[9]

The producers' support developed after Cannon's first victory in the Senate. Early in April, the former legislator had drafted a resolution authorizing a study of American trade with China. To avoid arousing any opposition, it did not mention silver. The Foreign Relations Committee chairman, William E. Borah, endorsed this resolution and another senior member of that committee, Key Pittman, offered it to the Senate on April 29, 1930, as a matter not needing discussion. Specifically, Senate Resolution 256 authorized the appointment of a subcommittee to the Committee on Foreign Relations to examine treaties involving American commercial relations with China and to study "conditions that may affect our commerce and trade" with that country. It was adopted without dissent the same day.[10]

Pursuant to the Senate resolution, Borah appointed a subcommittee and named Pittman chairman. The other members were Hiram Johnson of California, Arthur Vandenberg of Michigan, Claude Swanson of Virginia, and Henrik Shipstead of Minnesota. While Vandenberg and Johnson took little interest in this investigation, Swanson and Shipstead participated fully in the subcommittee's hearings that August and September.[11]

Pittman made no public announcement about the subcommittee's inquiry until early August. Then he explained that it would investigate the effect of the low price of silver on American export trade to China. He believed that declining prices adversely

43

affected this trade. The senator also released excerpts from written testimony submitted by Dr. Julius Klein, an undersecretary in the Department of Commerce, who stated that the major factors causing reduced exports to China were civil war in that country, generally lower commodity prices, and the low price of silver. Pittman argued that because the white metal's declining exchange value had reduced its purchasing power, China therefore needed greater quantities of the metal, particularly in its provincial interior.[12] The rebuttal to this contention was that China sold its commodities to purchase silver, rather than the reverse, and that imports from China had declined to a greater extent than American exports to that nation.[13] Also, its imports of silver largely resulted from a favorable balance of payments attributable to remittances from overseas Chinese.[14] Despite the weight of adverse opinion, Pittman said that declining prices and reduced exports justified a substantial loan to China.

Cannon assisted with the subcommittee's inquiry. He helped its staff gather data and locate witnesses. Following the hearings in Washington, he went to the West Coast and sought out exporters to testify at the sessions in Los Angeles and San Francisco. Much of their testimony lacked accuracy, however, and this reduced the impact of their frequent assertions that the low price of silver so affected Chinese purchasing power that it directly impaired the American export trade with that nation.[15]

Following the hearings in the Far West, Cannon and Pittman met with members of the International Silver Commission at Salt Lake City. They intended to coordinate agitation for a loan, but they disagreed over tactics. At one session, Senator Reed Smoot mentioned that he would support the plan in order to reelect Herbert Hoover. This displeased Pittman, who thereafter publicly identified himself as its main proponent.[16]

During the summer and fall months of agitation for the loan, some officials at Nanking, China, viewed it favorably. They heard of Cannon's scheme from Paul Myron W. Linebarger, an American sinophile who had been appointed legal advisor to the National government's Judicial Huan in April of 1930.[17] Before departing for Nanking, he had met with Cannon at the latter's request in Chicago.[18] Linebarger had readily agreed to present the idea to the Nationalists. His later writings indicated, moreover, that he strongly favored the plan and urged it upon his associates in China. He insisted that the silver should be used to establish road building projects in the interior, thereby occupying the time of the large numbers of former soldiers then without employment.[19]

The favorable attitude of some Chinese leaders toward the prospective loan had widened a split in China's Nationalist party. Supporters of the proposition were led by Hu Han-min, "the chief Rightist disciple and interpreter of Sun Yat-Sen," according to one authority.[20] The minister of finance, T. V. Soong, opposed any consideration of such a loan. His objections were based on the need for economy and the fact that the government already had a substantial load of debts. This quarrel came to a head after the council of state, without the prior approval of its president, General Chiang Kai-shek, issued a commission to Linebarger as a special envoy to negotiate the loan. Soong promptly resigned and demanded complete authority over financial matters as the price of his return.[21]

Chiang Kai-shek overruled those in the Nationalist party who favored the loan. His specific reasons were not announced, but he undoubtedly agreed with his brother-in-law, T. V. Soong, who quickly resumed his financial post.[22] A few months later Chiang removed Hu Han-min from the government due to the silver loan dispute and other unspecified "constitutional questions."[23] Meanwhile, Linebarger had sailed for San Francisco.

The government of China's American advisor learned late in October that his mission had been cancelled. Upon being informed by reporters that Soong had publicly questioned the proposed loan, Linebarger blandly said that he was only an advisor and that his advice might be rejected.[24] He made no further comment at that time about the division of opinion in Nanking. However, his later writing shows that he continued to regard Hu Han-min as the leading interpreter of the objectives espoused by Sun Yat-sen.[25]

Soon after learning that China had rejected the loan scheme,

45

Pittman lost interest in promoting the idea. When Cannon talked with him in Washington late the following month, Pittman said that while he still favored a loan, recent coversations with financial leaders in New York had convinced him of the need for international discussions of the project. These, he said, should precede any effort toward a loan of silver bullion.[26] Previously, Pittman had talked with Bernard Baruch, a member of American Smelting's board of directors, and Sir Charles Addis, board chairman of the Hong Kong and Shanghai Bank.[27]

Cannon slowly accepted the fact that his proposition had been rejected. Even into 1931, he continued to urge Borah to seek approval of a loan. Apparently, favorable editorial comment in the *New York Times* that January encouraged him to persevere. The following month, however, the report of Pittman's subcommittee on trade with China became public. It gave only mild approval to a loan of silver to China while strongly proposing American initiative to obtain international discussion of matters affecting the white metal.[28] Cannon ceased his agitation for the loan.

Cannon soon began a second drive to "do something for silver." His inspiration came from the European monetary debacle of that spring. On May 11, 1931, the Kreditanstalt Bank at Vienna failed. This started a series of economic crises which eventually forced many nations to abandon the gold standard.[29] These events intensified depression in the United States, where the American Farm Bureau Federation, for example, was demanding that something be done to stabilize the value of the dollar.[30] Concluding that it was time for all nations to return to bimetallism, Cannon decided to begin a campaign for its adoption by the United States.[31] That August he formed the Bimetallic Association. He became president, his stenographer, Miss Caroline Evans, became secretary, and his business associate, Robert C. Lane, treasurer. Although the association was a successor to the International Silver Commission, mining industry leaders in Salt Lake City and elsewhere withheld their support.[32]

Cannon hoped to involve the general public in his campaign. Membership in the Bimetallic Association was open to any person interested in the proposal, and the fee was nominal. The Junior Chamber of Commerce in Denver took a strong interest in this effort. Its members joined the association and urged their friends to follow suit. These young men arranged numerous speaking engagements for Cannon before various clubs and civic organizations in that region. The role of memberships increased steadily that fall but not as rapidly as its president desired.[33]

Cannon was not the sole advocate of bimetallism in the West. William Jennings Bryan, Jr., also began a drive to awaken interest in the remonetization of silver. The son of the Great Commoner began his agitation in California, where he was a practicing attorney. The younger Bryan believed, apparently, that the monetary crisis and swiftly advancing depression improved his chances as a political candidate. Like Burton K. Wheeler of Montana and others, Bryan aspired to be the Democrat's next vice-presidential nominee.[34]

Bryan and Cannon eventually joined forces. The former sought to organize a conference of persons interested in the white metal at some location in the producing regions. To this end he corresponded with officials in several of the mining states asking them to initiate the matter. Their joint efforts were destined to be more convenient than fortuitous in outcome.

Initially, Bryan hoped to convene a silver conference at Salt Lake City. He proposed that idea to George H. Dern, the governor of Utah, explaining that "this is the psychological moment for a campaign to effectively awaken the people to the need for the remonetization of silver." He proposed "a convention of all leaders interested in silver to meet the latter part of January at some convenient location." He meant Utah's capital city, but he did not choose to admit this to Dern.[35]

Governor Dern thought Bryan's plan unwise. He opposed reviving "Bryanism" in the West. This possibility repelled Dern both for its economic shortcomings and for its political impracticality. As a Democrat, he sought to avoid emotional issues that might lose votes in the coming presidential elections. The Democrats were a minority party in 1931, partly because of the Bryan heritage. In his reply, the governor told Bryan of the objectives

47

of those "who are specializing on this problem." He mentioned a recent conference of western governors at Portland, Oregon, where the silver question was discussed at length. The governors had adopted a resolution, Dern told the "go-it-alone" bimetallist, favoring an international conference on silver.[36]

Dern's answer enumerated reasons for delaying a silver conference in the West. He said that in light of the drive for an international assembly, nothing else should be attempted at that time. The governor also noted that a meeting in the West might interfere with the effort being made "to keep out partisanship of any sort." Finally, he reminded Bryan of the danger that silver's restoration might be interpreted as merely a selfish desire to benefit silver-producing states. Dern said that such a result would harm prospects for federal aid to the mining industry.[37]

The son of the Great Commoner was not dissuaded by the governor's objections. He had "received letters from almost every state in the Union" which indicated "a surprisingly widespread sentiment in favor of bimetallism." This response led Byran to disregard the governor's timidity. "The question of bimetallism . . . is already out," he said, and it would soon "become an economic issue in this country regardless of whether we want it or not."[38]

Dern attempted to block Bryan's scheme. He informed Democrats King and Pittman, but not Republican Reed Smoot, of the younger Bryan's intentions and of his persistence. Dern also wrote to the other Democratic governors in the West, encouraging them to oppose Bryan's plan for calling a western silver conference. He also went to California to persuade Bryan to change his plans, but again he failed.[39]

While Utah's governor opposed the calling of a conference, he was reluctant to say so officially. Dern had told Bryan of the strong opposition to his plan, but he had not answered the specific question. Bryan persisted, hinting that other governors had expressed interest. Finally, Dern said that he would not call a meeting because "an agitation for bimetallism at this time would injure rather than help [the] silver cause." The governor said that his view represented the attitude of W. Mont. Ferry and others who had been "the real leaders of the organized silver movement."[40] Ferry was a well-known Republican.

Pittman and King agreed with Dern's opposition to Bryan's plan. Pittman rejected the idea because the "east . . . is still bitterly prejudiced against what they call Bryanism." Moreover, he feared that agitation for bimetallism would only delay government action on silver.[41] King was opposed to having a conference in the West, but he thought a location in the Middle West would be acceptable. He believed, however, that bimetallism should not be the conference's declared goal.[42]

Despite Democratic opposition, Bryan's remonetization conference was held in the West. He won the help of Colorado's governor, William H. Adams, who issued an invitation to meet at Denver on February 15, 1932. Adams also appointed prominent Colorado citizens as delegates and provided a meeting place in the capitol.[43] Immediately before it began, Frank Cannon tried to foster a favorable climate in the host city. This silverite once had been editor of Denver's *Rocky Mountain News,* and now used that newspaper's columns liberally to publicize the event. It printed feature stories on William Jennings Bryan, Jr., as silver's new champion. Denver's Charles S. Thomas was photographed with Bryan and quoted as being pleased to see "a Bryan at the forefront of the silver movement again." These reports also mentioned that the Bimetallic Association was the local sponsor for the forthcoming conference.[44]

The advance publicity failed to generate enthusiasm. The efforts of Governor Adams, Frank Cannon, and William Jennings Bryan, Jr., were insufficient to overcome the apathy prevalent in the brief Western States Silver Conference. While the *Rocky Mountain News* reported approximately two hundred "delegates," most of these persons actually were observers. Only seventeen names were affixed to the "List of Registered Delegates."[45] After opening remarks by Morrison Shafroth, one of Colorado's leading political figures, Thomas E. Howard of the National Farmers' Union presented "with fire and fervor" a plea for the remonetization of silver.[46] Several others spoke to the same effect and in the early afternoon the conference adjourned.[47]

Bryan remained in Denver for several days. He issued a statement asserting that as chairman of the executive committee of the conference, he, in connection with the Bimetallic Association, would thereafter present the cause to the people in an "educational" and "non-partisan" way. Cannon heard little more from Bryan after his departure for California.[48]

In the weeks following the silver conference, the Bimetallic Association went into eclipse. Invitations for speeches became infrequent. Many people cancelled their pledges of support.[49] New memberships became a rarity. Despite a publicity drive in Colorado and surrounding states, membership fees totalled only $1,622 for the first twelve months, far less than the reported expenses for that period.[50] After mid-1932, bills went unpaid.[51] Thereafter, Cannon continued to advocate bimetallism, but the association retained few members and had no influence.[52] The association's secretary, Miss Caroline Evans, complained that because of the "screams going up from all over the country over the sales tax, the income tax, the wet or dry causes, our bimetallic pleas are mixed into the chaos."[53]

The senators from Colorado shared their constituents' disinterest in the Bimetallic Association. Edward P. Costigan had refused to join Cannon's organization even though he claimed to have "an abiding interest in silver."[54] His colleague, Alva B. Adams, flatly rejected the association's objective. He insisted, however, that he desired a substantial increase in prices for silver. Adams also said that he sought results rather than "merely championing a cause doomed to failure and seeking to secure approval at home."[55]

While the senators from Colorado seemed to be saying that they faced a condition and not a theory, such bimetallists as Frank J. Cannon sought to prove a theory and improve conditions as a result. They believed that restoration of silver would perfect the monetary system and thus insure a prompt and lasting return of prosperity and good feeling between classes and interests, except among those who controlled the gold. Like those who unyieldingly defended the yellow metal as a final measure of all things material, the adamant silverite sought an assured, lasting solution for a changing situation. Their cause was indeed "doomed to failure."

Between 1929 and 1932, Frank Cannon had twice failed to make significant headway in his campaigns to restore the white metal. He received aid from the producers in the first effort—to loan silver to China—but not in his second and even less fortunate drive for remonetization. An era had passed in the West but this believer in the "money metal" of another time had not changed his views.

The general public manifested little interest in bimetallism. Mining interests remained active in the West but their number and importance had markedly declined since the depression of the nineties. While general indifference blocked effective agitation, events on the national scene would soon restore the faith of many silverites. These individuals were found to be spread throughout the nation in the months following the 1932 elections. Their demands resounded in the national legislative halls and executive offices in Washington. The time had come to "do something for silver."

1. *Rocky Mountain News* (Denver), July 26, 1933; Caroline Evans, "Notes for Dr. Hafen," November 3, 1943, Cannon Papers, Biography folder; *Mines Register*, XIX (1937), 274.
2. Evans, "Notes," Cannon Papers, Biography folder.
3. Caroline Evans, "Some brief data" (ca. 1933), Cannon Papers, Data re Bimetallic Association folder.
4. *Ibid.* 5. *Ibid.*
6. Jo Ann Shipps, "The Mormons in Politics: The First Hundred Years" (Ph.D. dissertation, University of Colorado, 1965), pp. 244–49.
7. Evans, "Notes," November 3, 1943, Cannon Papers, Biography folder; *Mines Register*, XIX (1937), 876–78, 622–23.
8. Cannon to Gray Silver, May 17, 1930, Cannon Papers, Gray Silver folder; Brownell to Cannon, April 1, 1930, Correspondence, A–L folder. The other executive committee members were Cornelius F. Kelley of Anaconda, Frank Y. Robertson of United States Smelting, Refining and Mining, and Harold Hochschild of the American Metal Company.
9. Cannon to Robert C. Lane, August 16, 1931, Cannon Papers, Lane folder; Cannon to Jones, May 17, 1930, Cannon Papers, Gray Silver folder; *Engineering and Mining Journal*, CXXX (October 9, 1930), 354; Orville Merton Kile, *The Farm Bureau Through Three Decades* (Baltimore, Maryland: The Waverly Press, 1948), pp. 97–103.
10. U.S., *Congressional Record*, 71st Cong., 2d Sess., 1930, LXXII, Part 8

(April 29, 1930), 7930; Evans, "Some brief data" (ca. 1933), Cannon Papers, Data re Bimetallic Association folder.

11. U.S., Congress, Senate, Subcommittee of the Committee on Foreign Relations, *Hearings, Commercial Relations with China,* 71st Cong., 2d Sess., 1930, p. 1, *passim.*

12. *Ibid.,* pp. 2, 12; Pittman, news release, August 6, 1930, Pittman Papers, China trip folder; Israel, pp. 83–84. Opponents said China needed "dollars to be loaned by American bankers." *Engineering and Mining Journal,* CXXX (August 23, 1930), 196.

13. Bratter, "Silver," *Journal of Political Economy,* XXXIX, 349–51.

14. Wei-Ying Lin, *China Under Depreciated Silver, 1926–1931* (Shanghai: The Commercial Press, 1935), pp. 143–45.

15. U.S., Subcommittee of the Committee on Foreign Relations, *Hearings, Commercial Relations with China, passim;* Evans, "Notes," Cannon Papers, Biography folder.

16. Evans, "Notes," Cannon Papers, Biography folder.

17. Paul Myron W. Linebarger, *The Gospel of Chung Shan* (Paris: Brentano's, 1932), pp. 7–10.

18. Evans, "Notes," Cannon Papers, Biography folder.

19. Linebarger, *Gospel of Chung Shan,* pp. 191, 194.

20. Paul Myron Anthony Linebarger, *Government in Republican China* (New York: The McGraw Hill Book Company, 1938), p. 59.

21. *New York Times,* October 14, 15, 1930; Linebarger, *Gospel of Chung Shan,* p. 190.

22. *New York Times,* October 17, 1930.

23. Linebarger, *Government in Republican China,* p. 59; *New York Times,* March 2, 1931.

24. *New York Times,* November 1, 1930.

25. Linebarger, *Gospel of Chung Shan,* p. 194, *passim.*

26. Evans, "Notes," Cannon Papers, Biography folder.

27. Pittman to Baruch, November 11, 1930, Pittman Papers, "B" folder.

28. Cannon to Borah, January 12, 1931, February 23, 1931, Cannon Papers, Borah folder; *New York Times,* January 9, 1931; U.S., Congress, Senate, Committee on Foreign Relations, *Report, Commercial Relations with China,* Report No. 1716, 71st Cong., 3d Sess., 1931, p. 16.

29. Broadus Mitchell, *Depression Decade: From New Era Through New Deal, 1929–1941,* Vol. IX of *The Economic History of the United States,* ed. Henry David et al. (9 vols.; New York: Rinehart & Company, Inc., 1947), 11–12.

30. Joseph E. Reeve, *Monetary Reform Movements: A Survey of Recent Plans and Panaceas* (Washington: American Council on Public Affairs, 1943), pp. 10–12.

31. Evans, "Some brief data," Cannon Papers, Data re Bimetallic Association folder.

32. Cannon to Lane, August 1, 1931, Cannon Papers, Lane folder.

33. Caroline Evans to Horace S. Foster, October 17, 1931, Cannon Papers, U.S. Senators and Representatives folder; Memorandum on Speaking Engagements, no date, Cannon speeches and addresses folder.

34. Cannon to Russell F. Collins, February 19, 1932, Cannon Papers, Correspondence, F. J. Cannon folder.

35. Bryan to Dern, November 16, 1931, Dern Papers, box 44, International Silver Conference folder.

36. Dern to Bryan, December 7, 1931, Dern Papers, box 44, International Silver Conference folder.

37. *Ibid.*

38. Bryan to Dern, December 11, 1931, Dern Papers, box 44, International Silver Conference folder.

39. Dern to Bryan, December 12, 1931, Dern Papers, box 44, International Silver Conference folder.

40. Dern to Bryan, December 26, 30, 1931, Dern Papers, box 44, International Silver Conference folder.

41. Pittman to Dern, December 17, 1931, Dern Papers, box 46, Pittman folder.

42. King to Dern, December 4, 1931, Dern Papers, box 44, King folder.

43. *Denver Post,* January 19, 1932; February 14, 1932.

44. *Rocky Mountain News* (Denver), February 13, 14, 15, 1932; *Denver Post,* February 14, 1932.

45. "List of Registered Delegates, Western States Silver Conference," Cannon Papers, Convention, February 15, 1932, folder; *Rocky Mountain News* (Denver), February 16, 1932. The *News* reported that it was "a strange and motley gathering."

46. Cannon to Charles G. Binderup, July 23, 1932, Cannon Papers, Binderup folder.

47. *Rocky Mountain News* (Denver), February 16, 1932.

48. William Jennings Bryan, Jr., draft of statement, February 17, 1932, Cannon Papers, Convention, February 15, 1932, folder; Cannon to Russell F. Collins, February 19, 1932, Correspondence, A–L folder, both in the Cannon Papers. Bryan said that if $25,000 became available to open an office and begin a campaign in Washington, he too would be available.

49. Cannon to Frank J. Cook, June 30, 1932, Cannon Papers, Correspondence, F. J. Cannon, A–L folder.

50. "Statement of Receipts and Disbursements of the Bimetallic Association, Inc., August 12, 1931, to August 1, 1932, Cannon Papers, Letters to Executive Branch, U.S. Government folder. Membership totals did not exceed 600.

51. Caroline Evans to T. E. Bastina, December 5, 1932, Cannon Papers, Bimetallic Association folder.

52. *Ibid.*

53. Evans to Charles G. Binderup, June 2, 1932, Cannon Papers, Binderup folder.

54. Costigan to Cannon, August 28, 1931, Cannon Papers, Correspondence, U.S. Senate folder.

55. Adams to Evans, April 3, 1933, Cannon Papers, Correspondence, U.S. Senate folder.

4 Campaigning for Bimetallism

THE western silver producers' disinterest in agitation for bimetallism in 1932 contrasted with advances made in the following year. Interest revived in November after Franklin D. Roosevelt became president-elect, because silverites believed that he would be more amenable to such proposals than Herbert Hoover. By April, 1933, Senate backers of silver and inflation were sufficiently powerful to win discretionary authority to restore unlimited coinage. This dramatic reversal of fortunes for "free silver" came in concert with other grants of monetary power to aid Roosevelt in his efforts to "wage war" on depression.

In the months preceding the approval of bimetallism, advocates of this panacea made attractively high claims for it. They asserted that its reinstitution would revive American commerce and trade because it would expand the quantity of money serving as a basis of credit and increase the purchasing power of silver-using countries in Latin America and Asia. These arguments for remonetization, regardless of their merits when assessed objectively, were increasingly well received by many victims of the great depression.[1]

Burton K. Wheeler was the Silver Bloc's most outspoken proponent of independent American action to remonetize silver. In an article titled "The Silver Lining" published in 1932, he described the plight of those burdened with debt and he proposed bimetallism as the means to relieve their hardship. Wheeler claimed that the white metal was preferable to paper money as a means to obtain an increase in prices. He said that price inflation was necessary to provide a way to pay debts "with the same kind of dollar which we received when the debts were contracted." Also, the senator was absolutely certain that "we can pull our chariot out of the ditch of depression by harnessing silver to gold."[2] Wheeler was especially concerned in this article over the need to relieve farmers. At a later date he would come to question whether the nation could "materially help the farmer as long as forty-four countries are off the gold standard and we remain on it."[3] Generally, the senator looked to the needs of certain classes of people, while allowing others to perfect a smoothly functioning system.

Wheeler, Pittman, and Borah held differing views on the need to remonetize silver. Wheeler was the most reform-minded of the three, while Pittman was the least so inclined; between them ranged the frequently ambivalent "Lion of Idaho." While Pittman doubted "the wisdom of attempting to have two standards of measure for anything," Wheeler held that "any remedy which simply treats silver as a favored commodity will fail."[4] Both could find room for their views in Borah's stance.

I want a metallic basis for our money. It has been said that paper currency would be the most desirable money in the world if we could find someone with infinite wisdom to determine how much of it should be issued and under what circumstances. But that person does not exist.[5]

In the spring of that presidential election year, proponents and opponents of federal action on silver voiced their opinions before the House of Representatives' Committee on Coinage, Weights and Measures. Its chairman, Congressman Andrew L. Somers, a New York Democrat and an active promoter of remonetization and monetary inflation, began to investigate the "cause and effect of the present depressed value of silver."[6] He encouraged its partisans to express their views fully, and they frequently contradicted each other. Brownell of American Smelting asserted that the low price of silver had decreased American trade with the Orient, while Harold Hochschild of the American Metal Company said this matter had been greatly overemphasized.[7] Thus, even two members of the executive committee of the American Silver Producers' Association disagreed over the white metal's importance. In addition, bankers, economists, businessmen, and monetary theorists also added conflicting opinions.[8] These hearings increased public awareness of the silver issue in the weeks preceding the national political conventions.

In 1932, the monetary planks in the platforms of both major political parties included mention of silver. Secretary of the Treasury Ogden L. Mills presented the administration's draft to the Republican platform committee and it was adopted by the convention. As in 1896, that party made no commitment on silver other than to consider its position in relation to monetary questions at an international conference.[9] Senator Borah referred to it as "the betrayal of the silver question at Chicago."[10] The Democrats did not repeat their stand of 1896 for "free silver," but their plank was slightly more encouraging. It assured the preservation of a sound currency and pledged to begin action leading to an international monetary conference "to consider the rehabilitation of silver."[11] The platform committee rejected Senator Pittman's request for a promise to adopt silver purchase legislation.[12]

Silver advocates were disappointed with the monetary planks adopted by the major parties. A mining official in the Northwest, Frank M. Smith, expressed to Pittman the common feeling among silverites of regret tinged with impotence at being in a minority position. The planks were satisfactory as far as they had gone and there was "very little choice between them," he said, but it was evident to him that "the groups that controlled each convention were afraid of saying too much about silver."[13]

The reluctance of the national parties to emphasize the silver question brought contrasting reactions from Pittman and Borah. Pittman claimed to be satisfied. He reported to a leader of the Utah Mining Congress that he had "done everything" in his power "to keep this question out of politics."[14] Although a noted champion of the metal, he generally avoided words or deeds which might jeopardize the Democratic party's prospects. Borah, on the other hand, was dissatisfied. "There is no discussion of this subject whatever by either party," he complained, and to him that was "the most discouraging feature of the situation."[15] Subsequently, he made a series of speeches devoted to topics that the candidates "sedulously avoid."[16]

Finding little comfort in the 1932 party platforms, silver-conscious westerners turned to the presidential candidates to study their campaign behavior. Both nominees, Herbert Hoover and Franklin D. Roosevelt, were reluctant to discuss the silver question. Each mentioned this matter only when speaking in the mountain states.

Early in the campaign the Democratic nominee journeyed westward. His proposed remarks on silver were a matter of hot debate on the campaign train. Those arguments pitted three western senators against the candidate's advisors. One of the latter, Raymond Moley, later described the scene as a "struggle with the bimetallists on the train." These were Senators Pittman, Dill of Washington, and Thomas J. Walsh of Montana.[17] Moley indicated that the senators won the argument all too frequently. For example, Roosevelt deleted a phrase reading "we cannot submit to any plan which includes the remonetization of silver" from a draft prepared by his speech writers.[18]

Roosevelt emphasized the silver question in a speech at Butte, Montana. His main point was that he would initiate an international conference on silver immediately after being inaugurated. He also spoke of the need for improvement of conditions in the mining industry but he indicated that no single panacea would be sufficient. "The way out is difficult," Roosevelt said, "particularly with silver and the restoration of trade on the Pacific."[19] He offered hope to the silverites but he avoided unnecessary commitments.

Herbert Hoover avoided the subject until one of his last speeches as a political candidate. There were no silver senators on his train until it reached Salt Lake City. There, the president faced both his declining popularity in the West and the similar plight of Reed Smoot in Utah. Despite this, he made no promises about the white metal to entice mining votes. Hoover merely assured his listeners that an "increase in the value of silver would relieve us from strain." He also mentioned that governments should restore silver to greater use for "subsidiary coinage" and other traditional purposes. His fulsome praise for Reed Smoot and the Hawley-Smoot Act of 1930 contrasted sharply with his mild comments on silver.[20]

The election of Franklin D. Roosevelt unleashed a surge of inflationary expectations. The electorate had emphatically declared its distress over the depression by giving the Democrats the presidency and control of both houses of the Congress. Quickly, a rising clamor over the need to inflate prices gave the silver question a new prominence. However, its fate depended upon Roosevelt's policies after he assumed office.

The president-elect immediately became the focus of monetary debate. Authoritative voices urged him to defend the gold standard. The editors of a Boston newspaper questioned whether Roosevelt, who was under an election obligation to the inflationist states of the West and South, would oppose "the false gods of Bryan" in the manner of Grover Cleveland or surrender to the popular clamor.[21] Respected individuals such as Senator Carter Glass of Virginia, author of the Federal Reserve Banking Act, and formerly Woodrow Wilson's secretary of the Treasury, also advised restraint in Roosevelt's future monetary policies. Glass warned that "depreciation of the dollar will not raise commodity prices, but would so degrade our currency as to bring ruin to the wage earners and those on fixed salaries."[22]

While the debate over Roosevelt's future policies continued, Borah wrote several letters indicating the trend of his views. Early in 1933 he conceded the failure of current monetary policies. "Thus it is," he wrote, "we get neither currency inflation or credit inflation, and we are simply being driven into absolute collapse."[23] Nor could the imminent collapse be blamed on the westerners who were ready to act, Borah claimed, since "the overwhelming vote of the eastern states prevents effective action."[24] Borah's view was disarmingly simple. "I am in favor of a well thought out policy of inflation."[25] Furthermore, Borah was certain that the painful deflation of prices fully justified monetary experimentation. "I do not know how to raise the price of wheat and other

59

commodities except through some radical change in the present monetary system."[26]

Other members of the Silver Bloc were becoming inflationists. Arizona's senior senator, Henry F. Ashurst, announced his support for Wheeler's proposal for independent bimetallism because its enactment "would bring back prosperity in forty days."[27] Ashurst's colleague from Arizona, Carl Hayden, proposed a mildly inflationary silver plan in a nationally broadcast radio address.[28] Even the orthodox Reed Smoot vaguely asserted that inflation based on silver might be useful. "If we increase the price of silver and strengthen the money situation, it will employ tens of thousands of people and help the general situation tremendously."[29]

The public debate over inflation set the stage for testing sentiment in the Senate for remonetization. Some of the proposals advanced to bring about price inflation and to modify the nation's financial structure were so drastic as to make bimetallism appear safe and sane.[30] Increased support for remonetization in the South and Middle West soon became manifest in changing congressional attitudes. Developing interest in the white metal and inflation came at a fortunate time for the producers. On December 29, 1932, silver had closed at 24.25 cents per ounce on the bullion market at New York, the lowest price ever recorded for the metal.[31]

On January 24, 1933, Wheeler forced a vote on his bimetallism proposal. The measure then under discussion was the Glass-Steagall banking bill, a financial reform measure. Wheeler turned this situation to his advantage by introducing two amendments. As prearranged, Senator Huey P. Long of Louisiana offered the first of these.[32] It authorized a silver purchase program. Wheeler immediately offered his bimetallism plan as a substitute.[33] The Senate's rules required a vote on the substitution.

A lengthy debate preceded the vote on Wheeler's substitute measure. The most prominent voices in that discussion of bimetallism, inflation, prices, and related problems were those of Wheeler, Long, and Elmer Thomas of Oklahoma. Hours later, Glass protested that remonetization was not germane to his bill and requested that the former be tabled. The Senate agreed, fifty-six to eighteen.[34]

The vote to table Wheeler's amendment revealed a three-way division in the Silver Bloc. Six of the fourteen senators approved the motion to table, four opposed it, and four more failed to vote. The plurality favoring the motion included Republicans Smoot, Oddie, and John Thomas of Idaho; and Democrats Pittman, Hayden, and Sam G. Bratton of New Mexico. Those opposed to the tabling motion were Wheeler, Walsh, Ashurst, and Carl M. Schuyler of Colorado, an interim-term appointee. Borah, King, Costigan, and Bronson Cutting of New Mexico did not vote.[35] Wheeler promptly expressed his concern over some of those who voted to table, meaning Pittman, who "have always pretended . . . that they were for the remonetization of silver . . . when speaking to the voters."[36]

The eighteen votes to remonetize began a new alliance of silver and inflation forces. The two issues were rapidly becoming one. Of the eighteen senators opposed to tabling Wheeler's proposal, fourteen represented cotton, corn, and wheat growing states. This suggested a reemergence of the sectional voting patterns of the nineties—a political union west of the Mississippi and south of the Ohio.[37]

Wheeler, Pittman, and Borah varied sharply in their reactions to this vote. Wheeler claimed that the major mining and financial institutions opposed his amendment.

If the Guggenheim interests would take their heavy hand off the bill I've introduced . . . [it] might have a chance of passage. The great mining companies are openly opposed to the remonetization of silver because most of them are controlled by the big banking interests of New York.[38]

Pittman emphasized the futility of Wheeler's strategy. "Every western senator, except two, begged Wheeler not to offer his bill," Pittman told a friend, adding his belief that "it has not any chance of passage at this session or any other session for years. . . ."[39] Pittman objected to the entire procedure, saying "we should not do anything to frighten the gold standard people, be-

61

cause they still have a majority in Congress."[40] While Pittman rejected Wheeler's strategy, Senator Borah renounced national bimetallism as a policy. He candidly told a constituent that "if we get behind the Wheeler bill, which in effect abandons the fight for international adjustment, we will practically abandon the cause of silver."[41]

While the senators viewed the situation as complex, some constituents took a simple, direct approach. These persons were disturbed by the fragmented vote on the Wheeler amendment. They accepted no deviation from loyalty to the white metal. One of them wrote from Tonopah to Pittman plaintively asking

> . . . how you and Senator Oddie could bring yourselves to vote against the Wheeler silver bill. Even if it had no chance to pass at this session it certainly looks strange to see both senators from a silver state voting against it. . . . Like many other of your constitutents I find it difficult to understand your votes on silver.[42]

Even before the vote on bimetallism, the constituents had taken action that incidentally made the Silver Bloc more cohesive. In the 1932 elections they had increased the Democratic majority from eight to twelve. Those not reelected were Reed Smoot, Tasker L. Oddie, John Thomas of Idaho, and Charles W. Waterman of Colorado, all Republicans. The Republicans remaining in office were Borah and Cutting, while the continuing Democrats were Pittman, Wheeler, King, Hayden, Ashurst, Costigan, and Bratton; John S. Erickson of Montana was appointed to fill the seat vacated when Walsh died. The newly elected members of the Bloc were Elbert D. Thomas of Utah, Patrick A. McCarran of Nevada, James P. Pope of Idaho, and Alva B. Adams of Colorado.[43]

The Silver Bloc steadily augmented its power and influence during the first years of the New Deal. This resulted from a combination of circumstances. The nation was ready to experiment with new ideas and old panaceas intended to improve economic conditions. Inflationists in the Farm Bloc approved and even sponsored silver legislation. The senators' differences of opinion were subordinated to satisfy constituents interested in mining and its prosperity. The Bloc was ably led by Pittman, who was also chairman of the Senate's Committee on Foreign Relations and its president pro tempore.[44] Finally, perhaps of more importance than the foregoing, Franklin D. Roosevelt sought to restore the economy through aid to industry, agriculture, and labor. He did not object to a subsidy for mining interests.

Following his inauguration on March 4, 1933, the new president called Congress into special session to cope with the banking crisis then threatening the nation's financial system. Five days later it swiftly adopted the measures proposed by the chief executive. These resolved the emergency if not the underlying problems, and the Congress remained in session for the following three months. During that period it adopted many other important measures, including aid to agriculture.

Senator Wheeler seized a second opportunity to advance bimetallism during the Senate's debates on legislation to restore agriculture to its prewar affluence. The president's endorsement of that goal encouraged inflationists to amend the administration's bill to include monetary means to raise prices.[45]

Wheeler's second attempt to obtain remonetization came in mid-April. By then, the House of Representatives had approved the Agricultural Adjustment bill; although it had cleared the Senate's Committee on Agriculture, it was halted by extended debate on the floor. Wheeler and a number of his colleagues announced their intention to amend the measure.[46] The senator said that even if it was later defeated, the vote would "impress the President and convince him that it would be wise to take an active part in promoting some silver legislation."[47] Pittman again dismissed Wheeler's initiative as a futile exercise. "A casual poll of the . . . Senate indicates that two-thirds of [the senators] will be against the Wheeler bill . . . ."[48]

On April 17, 1933, the Senate devoted an entire legislative day to the silver question. This was more than a mere repetition of the previous skirmish. A weekend of intensive political activity and newspaper comment preceded this clash over "free silver." Another difference appeared in the debate. During the hours of tedious argument, Borah, Pittman, and King vigorously supported the principle of bimetallism, although Borah and Pittman carefully avoided an endorsement of the Wheeler bill.[49] Unchanged, however, was the heated controversy pitting Wheeler and Elmer Thomas against their leading opponents, Senators Reed of Pennsylvania and Townsend of Delaware.[50]

The activity controlling prospects for adoption of the Wheeler amendment transpired in the Senate's cloakrooms. There, the Democratic leadership strained to reduce the favorable vote. This tactic led a dozen or more of the western and southern Democrats to telephone the president's legislative liaison, Raymond Moley, to explain their political difficulties. He advised them to be absent on the roll call, then to enter the chamber and vote "nay" if the favorable vote tally had reached thirty. If not, they were free to vote "yea" for the "folks back home."[51]

Despite pressures by Democratic leaders, the vote on "free silver" was unexpectedly close, thirty-three to forty-four, with nineteen not voting.[52]

While only a third of the senators approved the bill, less than half voted against it. Apparently, a majority favored some form of inflation, if not the Wheeler amendment. The vote told the Roosevelt administration that it must cope with congressional demands for inflation.

The balloting on "free silver" had an unexpected aftermath which startled the Democratic leadership. Immediately following the vote, Elmer Thomas offered a measure that combined several well-known ideas into one politically powerful compendium.[53] It included his own paper money scheme,[54] Wheeler's bimetallism amendment, and a plan to reduce the dollar's gold content. The last mentioned proposal, similar to one introduced previously by Tom Connally of Texas, was then lying on the Senate table.[55] Thomas had made an important change in each of the foregoing measures, however, because he asked that the president be authorized, but not required, to undertake monetary inflation. As the senator specifically intended, he at once united the competing inflationist groups.[56]

The senator from Oklahoma acted less precipitously than it

seemed at the time. He had long demanded monetary relief to aid the nation's farmers.[57] Also, his amendment specifically fulfilled two objectives endorsed at the Democratic party's Farm Conference held in December, 1932. Guided by the president-elect's farm policy advisors—including Henry Wallace, Rexford Tugwell, and Henry Morgenthau—it made specific recommendations on monetary policy. These called for both complete federal control of the monetary system and controlled monetary inflation.[58] Roosevelt had ignored these recommendations in his agricultural bill.

Thomas had sought to correct this omission through action by the Senate Committee on Agriculture. It rejected Thomas' inflation amendment but only due to its lack of jurisdiction on monetary matters. The committee had amended the president's bill, however, to include a lengthy, vigorous endosement of the principle of monetary inflation.[59]

On April 12, 1933, Thomas introduced his inflation plan as an amendment to the agricultural bill, asking that it be printed and permitted to lie on the table.[60] This procedure was unusual. Had he followed accepted practice, his amendment would have been buried by the Banking and Currency Committee.

The Thomas amendment caused a sensation. Immediately after a clerk completed its oral reading, Majority Leader Joseph Robinson of Arkansas ended debate. Impressive support emerged within hours.[61] Organized inflationists contributed to the clamor. Dozens of western farmers demanding monetary relief had descended on Washington at the behest of John A. Simpson, president of the National Farmers' Union.[62] The Committee for the Nation to Rebuild Prices and Purchasing Power also strongly supported Thomas' inflationary measure.[63]

The strength of the amendment's supporters prompted the administration to reassess the situation. Informed opinion was unanimous; the amendment could easily pass both houses of Congress. Senate leaders, presidential advisors, even political columnists Walter Lippmann and Arthur Krock agreed. For proof, observers pointed to those voting "nay" on remonetization. The number even included several known inflationists, Connally, Borah, and others. Moley took this information to the president.[64]

On April 18, 1933, Roosevelt decided to accept the Thomas amendment. Its opponents failed to change his mind. The popular clamor for monetary action overrode the best judgment of his associates.[65] Of these, only Budget Director Lewis Douglas asserted his opposition vigorously. James P. Warburg, another "sound money" advisor and the scion of a famous banking family, later wrote that "no one, as far as I know, in administration circles, unless it was the President himself, had any idea" that previous monetary policies would be altered.[66] Later, Warburg referred to the Thomas amendment as "an exceedingly narrow squeak."[67] His comment supported Moley's overall assessment, since the latter credited pure circumstance—"the prosaic results of a counting of noses in the Senate"[68]—as being the decisive factor. He later said of these events that "rationalizations—the business of making a virtue of necessity—came after the decisions were made."[69]

The president's views on the Thomas amendment were not recorded at that time. Arthur Schlesinger, Jr., has noted that the president "could only give a fraction of his attention to monetary questions." He also suggests that the president's attitude on monetary matters seemed to express "a heretical feeling that on some issues Elmer Thomas might be nearer right than Lewis Douglas." Like Roosevelt's advisors, Schlesinger had to speculate on this point. Warburg later complained that he was not "able to pin the man down so that he would really think about it—a very odd experience."[70]

Prior to April 18, the most precise indication of Roosevelt's attitude appeared in his letter of April 5 to Colonel Edward M. House: "It is simply inevitable that we must inflate and though my banker friends will be horrified, I am still seeking an inflation which will not wholly be based on additional government debt."[71]

On the afternoon of April 18, the president and Senator Thomas agreed to a truce. According to the Senator's memoirs, he explained the "conveniences" of the powers granted by his amendment to Roosevelt. Thomas emphasized, he later wrote, that Senate ratification of any international monetary agreement negotiated at the prospective Monetary and Economic Conference would not be necessary, since the president would be delegated "all power over money."[72] At length, he claimed, they struck a bargain. The president promised to back the amendment and Thomas agreed to "minor changes" by Roosevelt's advisors, providing that their draft retained provision for presidential control.[73]

Roosevelt's decision to accept inflation was disputed by his advisors. He met with them on the evening of April 18 to discuss the forthcoming world economic conference. He opened the session by telling them he had decided to support the Thomas amendment and to abandon the gold standard. Immediately, "hell broke loose" in the room, according to Moley, followed by two hours of intense discussion of monetary policy. Key Pittman was present and defended both of the president's decisions.[74]

The next day, Moley, Warburg, Douglas, and Pittman reworked the Thomas amendment. Their labors began that morning in the Committee on Foreign Relations' conference room and ended late that night in Moley's apartment. The new draft retained optional authority to issue greenbacks, but limited the amount to three billion dollars. While it permitted the president to fix the weight of the gold and the silver dollars and to establish the ratio of silver to gold, it eliminated Thomas' unlimited coinage provision and his pet idea, a dollar stabilization board.

The revised Thomas amendment bore evidence of Pittman's influence. It permitted the Treasury, at the president's discretion, to accept limited amounts of silver at no more than fifty cents per ounce in payment of obligations due the United States from foreign governments for a period of six months after enactment. It further provided authority to coin standard silver dollars from such silver and to issue silver certificates backed by the silver dollars retained in the Treasury.[75]

Thomas introduced the new draft on April 20, but he remained wary. Before submitting his revised amendment to the Senate's procedures, he extracted a promise from Florida's Duncan U. Fletcher, chairman of the Committee on Banking and Currency,

67

that the proposal would be reported to the floor by noon of the following day.[76] Fletcher reported the amendment to the Senate with only minor changes within the alloted time.[77]

Wheeler, on learning that authority for the unlimited coinage of silver was being eliminated from the Thomas amendment, threatened to "raise some cain" in the Senate. His informant was Elmer Thomas' good friend, Father Charles E. Coughlin, the radio-priest, who was then visiting in Washington. Wheeler bitterly criticized Roosevelt in Coughlin's presence.[78]

Wheeler's outburst led to a compromise. Apparently, the White House learned from Coughlin of the senator's threatening words. The following day, presidential secretary Marvin McIntyre persuaded Wheeler, who professed reluctance, to talk with Roosevelt. At a meeting on April 20, the latter listened patiently to Wheeler's complaint that he had been excluded from the group that rewrote the Thomas amendment and eliminated authority for "free silver." In reply, Roosevelt said that "Bryan killed remonetization of silver" and he could not be for it. Undaunted, Wheeler insisted that he would offer his measure again to Congress.[79] Meanwhile, Senator King entered the president's office and joined the conversation. With King inclining toward Roosevelt's position, they continued to discuss the remonetization bill with him. Finally, Roosevelt told them to submit an amendment to him.[80]

Wheeler won his objective, at least in part. The authority for bimetallism would be restored but the remonetization of silver remained one step away. While the senator originally had sought mandatory restoration at the legal ratio of 15.988 to 1, silver to gold (but often referred to as "sixteen to one"), he actually attained permissive authority for remonetization at a ratio of the president's choosing.

Working with King, Wheeler quickly found a way to include the remonetization in the Thomas amendment. In the section which authorized the president to fix the weight of the gold and silver dollars, they added the words "and to provide for the unlimited coinage of such gold and silver at the ratio so fixed." After presenting this modification to Roosevelt, they submitted a copy to the Senate.[81] That body approved the Wheeler-King amendment by a vote of forty-one to twenty-six, with twenty-seven not voting. The measure carried on its own strength, since Roosevelt refused to take a public position on the question.[82] His attitude may explain the large number of nonvoters. Included in that group were Pittman, Borah, Costigan, and Ashurst; the twelve remaining silver senators voted for unlimited coinage of the white metal.[83]

Despite assertions that an inflationary spiral would ensue, the Senate approved the Thomas amendment by a vote of sixty-four to twenty-one.[84] The decisive majority for the measure perhaps justified an earlier remark by Thomas that "they've got the generals, but we've got the privates."[85] The editor of a newspaper in New Orleans suggested that this vote had historical significance —one perhaps more apparent in the South and the West than in eastern centers of affairs. He said: "The vote will constitute, as a whole, the greatest test of the mastery of money against service to the people which has taken place since Jackson asserted the sovereignty of the people against the money power."[86] This interpretation of the fight for monetary relief was commonplace in the South and West.

The practical effect of the Thomas amendment depended upon one inscrutable man, Franklin D. Roosevelt. That fact boosted confidence among inflationists. The president had indicated a disposition toward monetary inflation when he decided to abandon the gold standard as a permanent policy. His decision portended, so it seemed to observers (some fearfully, others hopefully), a policy of monetary experimentation intended to expand the currency and to raise commodity prices. For the time being, this measure pacified inflationists in the Senate.

The Thomas amendment was a triumph for the Silver Bloc. Congress had provided the power to remonetize silver and to accept that metal in payment of war debts. Like the agrarian inflationists, the Silver Bloc was an early beneficiary of the New Deal.

69

1. Leavens, *Silver Money*, pp. 236–43.
2. Burton K. Wheeler, "The Silver Lining," *Liberty*, IX (October 22, 1932), 15–16.
3. *Rocky Mountain News* (Denver), March 24, 1933.
4. U.S., House of Representatives, Committee on Coinage, Weights and Measures, *Hearings, Silver Money*, 72d Cong., 2d Sess., 1933, pp. 40, 60.
5. Borah to Richard Lloyd Jones, January 18, 1933, Borah Papers, box 344, Currency folder.
6. U.S., *Congressional Record*, 72d Cong., 1st Sess., 1931, LXXV, Part 1 (December 18, 1931), 898.
7. U.S., Congress, House of Representatives, Committee on Coinage, Weights and Measures, *Hearings, The Effects of Low Silver*, 72d Cong., 1st Sess., 1932, pp. 40, 53–54, 56.
8. *Ibid.*
9. *New York Times*, June 16, 1932. Text of platform, p. 15. In 1896, the Republican party had taken a similar position by rejection of bimetallism except in concert with "the leading nations . . . which agreement we pledge ourselves to promote." Paul W. Glad, *McKinley, Bryan and the People* (Philadelphia: J. B. Lippincott Company, 1964), p. 110.
10. Borah to A. D. Kelley, June 29, 1932, Borah Papers, box 340, Silver folder.
11. *New York Times*, June 30, 1932. Text of platform, p. 15.
12. Pittman to Brownell, June 27, 1932, Pittman Papers, box 140, "B" folder. In 1896 the Democrats had promised the free and unlimited coinage of silver and gold and had nominated William Jennings Bryan to carry out that promise if elected. Paolo E. Coletta, *William Jennings Bryan, I, Political Evangelist 1860–1908* (Lincoln, Nebraska: University of Nebraska Press, 1964), pp. 129, 143, 146.
13. Smith to Pittman, July 7, 1932, Pittman Papers, box 145, "S" folder.
14. Pittman to A. G. Mackenzie, July 16, 1932, Pittman Papers, box 144, "M" folder.
15. Borah to J. H. Sawtelle, August 24, 1932, Borah Papers, box 340, Silver folder.
16. *New York Times*, October 13, 1932.
17. Raymond P. Moley, *After Seven Years* (New York: Harper & Brothers, 1939), p. 57. Later Thomas J. Walsh was Roosevelt's choice for attorney general, but he died before the inauguration.
18. *Ibid.* 19. *New York Times*, September 20, 1932.
20. *Ibid.*, November 8, 1932.
21. *Boston Evening Transcript*, January 23, 1933.
22. *Rocky Mountain News* (Denver), January 24, 1933.
23. Borah to G. S. States, February 6, 1933, Borah Papers, box 344, Currency folder.
24. Borah to James Cornell, February 8, 1933, Borah Papers, box 344, Currency folder.
25. Borah to S. R. Walton, March 31, 1933, Borah Papers, box 344, Currency folder.
26. Borah to M. A. Driscol, January 2, 1933, Borah Papers, box 344, Currency folder.
27. *Denver Post*, January 23, 1933.
28. *New York Times*, December 27, 1932.
29. *Rocky Mountain News* (Denver), January 8, 1933.

30. Jeanette P. Nichols, "Silver Inflation and the Senate in 1933," *The Social Studies,* XXV (January, 1934), 13.

31. Leavens, *Silver Money,* p. 141.

32. U.S., *Congressional Record,* 72d Cong., 2d Sess., 1933, LXXVI, Part 2 (January 23, 1933), 2293.

33. *Ibid.,* p. 2294. 34. *Ibid.,* Part 3 (January 24, 1933), 2349, 2393.

35. *Ibid.,* pp. 2392–93. 36. *Ibid.,* p. 2394.

37. *Ibid.,* pp. 2393–94; Cooley, "Silver Politics," p. 103. One of these senators, J. Hamilton Lewis, represented Illinois.

38. U.S., *Congressional Record,* 72d Cong., 2d Sess., 1933, LXXVI, Part 2 (January 25, 1933), 2465.

39. Pittman to Lee F. Hand, February 24, 1933, Pittman Papers, box 143, "H" folder.

40. Pittman to Ray Kingsburg, February 10, 1933, Pittman Papers, box 144, "K" folder.

41. Borah to Axel Ramstedt, March 10, 1933, Borah Papers, box 353, Silver folder.

42. Lee F. Hand to Pittman, February 20, 1933, Pittman Papers, box 143, "H" folder.

43. U.S., *Congressional Directory,* 73d Cong., 1st Sess., June, 1933, pp. 5–6; 13; 22–23; 62–63; 65; 70–71; 117.

44. *Ibid.,* p. 65. The date was March 19, 1933.

45. For a complete discussion of these events see Arthur M. Schlesinger, Jr., *The Age of Roosevelt,* Vol. II, *The Coming of the New Deal* (Boston: Houghton Mifflin Company, 1959), pp. 40–42.

46. U.S., *Congressional Record,* 73d Cong., 1st Sess., 1933, LXXVII, Part 2 (April 14, 1933), 1741–42.

47. *Salt Lake Tribune,* April 15, 1933. This article, written by a special correspondent in Washington, listed several reasons for opposing the bill and mentioned that several of the silver senators were fearful of the stigma of Bryanism.

48. Pittman to A. L. Scott, March 14, 1933, Pittman Papers, box 144, Legislatures and Governments folder.

49. U.S., *Congressional Record,* 73d Cong., 1st Sess., 1933, LXXVII, Part 2 (April 17, 1933), 1817, 1841.

50. *Ibid.,* 1741. 51. Moley, *After Seven Years,* p. 158.

52. U.S., *Congressional Record,* 73d Cong., 1st Sess., 1933, LXXVII, Part 2 (April 17, 1933), 1842. Twelve silver senators voted for the amendment. Opposed were Hayden and Bratton (as in January), and Borah. The latter so voted, he said, to satisfy the president. Pittman did not vote due to a special pair with Carter Glass.

53. U.S., *Congressional Record,* 73d Cong., 1st Sess., 1933, LXXVII, Part 2 (April 12, 1933), 1537.

54. *Ibid.,* 72d Cong., 2d Sess., 1932, LXXVI, Part 1 (December 23, 1932), 949. Thomas offered a bill (S. 5292) to authorize the Treasury to pay current government expenses with "liberty notes," a new paper currency.

55. *Ibid.,* 73d Cong., 1st Sess., 1933, LXXVIII, Part 1 (April 3, 1933), 1103; *New York Times,* March 24, 1933.

56. Elmer Thomas to author, May 20, 1963. Senator Thomas firmly maintains that he alone composed the Thomas amendment. No one else, including his old friends John A. Simpson and George A. LeBlanc, a Wall Street investment specialist, aided the senator.

57. Elmer Thomas, "Forty Years a Legislator" (Elmer Thomas Papers,

University of Oklahoma Library Division of Manuscripts, Norman, Oklahoma), p. 226. Hereafter cited as E. Thomas Papers.

58. John M. Blum, *From the Morgenthau Diaries*, I, *Years of Crisis, 1928–1938* (Boston: Houghton Mifflin Company, 1959), pp. 39–41.

59. U.S., Congress, Senate, Committee on Agriculture, *Report, Relieve the Existing National Economic Emergency by Increasing Agricultural Purchasing Power*, 73d Cong., 1st Sess., 1933, Report No. 16, p. 6; Thomas, "Forty Years a Legislator," p. 226.

60. U.S., *Congressional Record*, 73d Cong., 1st Sess., 1933, LXXVII, Part 2 (April 12, 1933), 1537.

61. Moley, *After Seven Years*, pp. 158–59. Early the following morning Democrats Bulkley of Ohio and Byrnes of South Carolina phoned Moley to warn him that the Thomas amendment would sweep through the Senate.

62. *New York Times*, April 11, 1933.

63. Schlesinger, *Coming of the New Deal*, pp. 198–99. "The Committee lent a sort of pseudo-respectability to the inflation drive."

64. Moley, *After Seven Years*, pp. 158–59; *New York Times*, April 18, 19, 1933.

65. Moley, *After Seven Years*, p. 57.

66. James P. Warburg, *The Money Muddle* (New York: Alfred A. Knopf, 1934), p. 96. Warburg was an unpaid assistant without portfolio from March through October, 1933.

67. Israel, p. 102.   68. Moley, *After Seven Years*, p. 157.

69. *Ibid.*, p. 161; Moley, *First New Deal*, p. 304. For an excellent general assessment, see Schlesinger, *Coming of the New Deal*, pp. 194–201.

70. Schlesinger, *Coming of the New Deal*, pp. 202–203.

71. Elliott Roosevelt (ed.), *F. D. R., His Personal Letters*, III (New York: Duell, Sloan and Pearce, 1959), 342.

72. Thomas, "Forty Years a Legislator," p. 230.

73. *Ibid.;* Moley, *After Seven Years*, p. 159. For conflicting views between Moley and Thomas see respectively: Moley, *First New Deal*, pp. 300–01; U.S., *Congressional Record*, 73d Cong., 1st Sess., 1933, LXXVII, Part 2 (April 17, 1933), 1844.

74. Schlesinger, *Coming of the New Deal*, pp. 200–01; Moley, *After Seven Years*, pp. 159–60; Moley, *First New Deal*, pp. 302–03; Herbert Feis, *1933: Characters in Crisis* (Boston: Little, Brown and Company, 1966), pp. 127–30. These accounts conflict but the most complete and accurate is that by Feis. He attended as economic advisor to the State Department. Feis cites James P. Warburg's Journal for April 18, 1933, as the source for one contradiction of Moley's account.

75. U.S., *Congressional Record*, 73d Cong., 1st Sess., 1933, LXXVII, Part 2 (April 20, 1933), 1844, 2003.

76. *Ibid.*, pp. 2003–04.   77. *Ibid.* (April 22, 1933), p. 2170.

78. Burton K. Wheeler to author, September 22, 1961.

79. *Ibid.;* Wheeler quoted Roosevelt's remark on Bryan during an interview on September 17, 1962.

80. *Ibid.*

81. U.S., *Congressional Record*, 73d Cong., 1st Sess., 1933, LXXVII, Part 2 (April 24, 1933), 2246.

82. Burton K. Wheeler to author, September 22, 1961. Majority leader Robinson told Wheeler of this, but Robinson also told Wheeler to go ahead and offer the amendment.

83. U.S., *Congressional Record*, 73d Cong., 1st Sess., 1933, LXXVII, Part

3 (April 28, 1933), 2551–52. Cooley has suggested that Pittman and Borah were likely detained from the Senate due to conferences with British officials then in Washington with Ramsay MacDonald.

84. *Rocky Mountain News* (Denver), April 23, 1933. Thomas was quoted by Lyle C. Wilson, a reputable United Press newsman, but the quote may be an enterprising invention.

85. U.S., *Congressional Record,* 73d Cong., 1st Sess., 1933, LXXVII, Part 2 (April 26, 1933), 2410.

86. U.S., *Congressional Record,* 73d Cong., 1st Sess., 1933, LXXVII, Part 3 (April 26, 1933), 2401. Originally published in *New Orleans Item,* April 25, 1933.

5 A Subsidy for Silver

During 1933, Senator Key Pittman urged the Treasury Department to buy domestically produced silver. His activities were varied, persistent, and ultimately persuasive. He sought legislation during the spring, and that summer became a delegate to the London Economic Conference. There, Pittman negotiated agreements helpful to silver producers with delegates representing eight nations. Later the president ratified these accords by exercising his emergency monetary powers. The senator's efforts were effective because he strove for attainable objectives.

Despite criticism by constituents, most western senators were realists on the silver issue, and Pittman was the most persistent. His efforts that year to secure silver purchases were sharply criticized by some westerners, who said his willingness to compromise would prevent remonetization. The senator answered a complaint from Jonathan Bourne, a former colleague from Oregon and a Progressive Republican who prompted Wheeler to advocate bimetallism.[1] Pittman admitted that his theory of legislation was one of compromise: "I would rather take one step at a time, than eternally fall through an attempted too broad a jump."[2]

Within a month after Roosevelt's inauguration, Pittman began working for an agreement between the new administration and the Silver Bloc. On April 5, 1933, he was host at a private dinner for legislators and presidential advisors. Pittman's gathering honored William H. Woodin, Roosevelt's amiable and able secretary of the Treasury. Also present were seventeen members of

75

the Congress, each having introduced silver legislation during the preceding thirty days, including Assistant Secretary of State Raymond Moley, who acted as the president's legislative liaison. Each legislator had an opportunity to explain his ideas to Woodin. Pittman encouraged the secretary to select the proposal most compatible with monetary policies then being formulated. The measures proposed were both intricate and controversial, however, and Woodin refused to be committed.[3]

Despite his persistence and seeming single-mindedness, Pittman used rational and effective techniques to achieve his legislative goals. He listened to and shared credit with his colleagues. These traits plus his personal qualities assured his welcome among Roosevelt's advisors and assistants.[4] These persons were comparatively inexperienced in Washington, where Pittman had been acquiring expertise for nearly twenty years. Furthermore, he was an able, persuasive legislator, well versed on his objective—the rehabilitation of silver—and knew how to achieve it, so long as Roosevelt did not bar the way. The latter's commanding prestige during the early period of his administration prevented legislative action which he outspokenly opposed. Later events indicated that the senator never overlooked that fact.

Pittman began his drive for silver legislation on March 9, 1933, the first day of the special session known as the "100 days" Congress, by introducing three proposals. Senate Bill 145 permitted the Treasury to accept silver in lieu of gold from foreign governments as installments on war debts due the United States government. Senate Bill 146 authorized the Treasury to make limited purchases from current domestic production. Senate Bill 147 authorized the Treasury to buy on the world market. The purchase programs would be self-supporting; silver certificates were to be issued as payment for the silver, and the silver coined into silver dollars and held for redemption of the circulating paper.[5] None of these measures became law, although the ideas turned up later in other pieces of legislation.

Pittman's proposal on war debt installments sought to alleviate a controversial situation. The debtor governments wanted cancellation, and American opinion was divided over this proposition. Observers thought the Congress was opposed. The issue produced an impasse between Hoover and Roosevelt during the interim between election day and the latter's inauguration in March.[6] In 1933, international enmity over these debts seemed likely to create a political issue in the United States.

Pittman's payment proposal resulted from a study made by Senator Carl Hayden. In 1932, the latter had surveyed the coinage practices of debtor governments. Hayden found that since 1920 each had reduced its silver coinage in some manner. In his introduction to the Senate document on this matter, dated April 4, 1933, Hayden said that in his opinion, two outstanding facts are shown by this report:

First. That without a proper realization of the ultimate effect upon price levels throughout the world, nation after nation, to gain a temporary advantage for itself, has in recent years debased or demonetized its silver coinage. The silver thus obtained has been thrown upon the market driving the price of that metal to the lowest point in all recorded time, with repercussions which have been felt in every avenue of trade.

Second. That since 1900 there also has been a reduction of over two-thirds in the use of silver by central banks as a reserve against issues of paper money. Instead of using silver as a handmaiden to gold, a greater burden has thus been placed upon the yellow metal with a consequent enhancement of its value.[7]

The silver payments plan played a brief role in Anglo-American relations. Pittman and Hayden wrote its essentials into the Thomas amendment.[8] The fact that only six nations—Finland, Czechoslovakia, Italy, Lithuania, Rumania, and Great Britain— paid debt installments on June 15, 1933, reduced its importance. Each country exercised its option of utilizing silver.[9] Their token payments—the silver bullion was arbitrarily valued at fifty cents per ounce by the United States—came during the Monetary and Economic Conference. The British probably hoped that this payment, their last, would quiet Anglophobes and silverites during the talks in London. Pittman, while mindful of both groups,

77

announced that the British action constituted "the greatest encouragement to the intrinsic value of the [white] metal ever announced."[10]

The League of Nations sponsored the Monetary and Economic Conference held at London that June, pursuant to requests from the European nations that had met a year earlier at Lausanne, Switzerland, to discuss reparations and war debts. The United States had not been represented at that conference. Before it met, however, the Hoover administration had accepted a British invitation to begin planning for a later conference on general economic and monetary problems, excluding the topics of war debts and reparations. Hoover's acceptance stipulated that the agenda include the silver problem.[11]

In April, 1933, Roosevelt asked Pittman to be a delegate and he readily accepted, thereafter assisting the president's advisors in devising statements on gold and silver consonant with the unorthodox presidential views. Raymond Moley later informed Roosevelt that "Pittman is [the] only member of [the] delegation able intellectually and aggressively to present your ideas."[12]

Pittman prepared for the London Economic Conference through preliminary conversations with prospective foreign delegates who visited Washington that April and May. His efforts centered on representatives from the nations most concerned with silver: Great Britain, Canada, Mexico, and China.[13] Pittman carefully solicited the opinions and intentions of T. V. Soong, China's minister of finance. Soong favored silver agreements such as the senator hoped to propose.[14] Later, at London, Soong publicly praised Pittman's efforts and expressed the hope that the Economic Conference would thereafter attempt to "raise and stabilize the price of silver, thus increasing the purchasing power of China and India."[15]

The preliminary conversations led to a tentative understanding. According to Pittman, Great Britain, Canada, Mexico, and China sought a common goal. Their delegates agreed to request that all nations discontinue the practice of debasing their silver coinage, and if debasement had already taken place, to restore their coinage to its former purity. Concerted action, Pittman believed, would not only enhance silver's monetary status, but also help raise its price. The senator also had urged, without success, that the nations most concerned make agreements to stabilize the price of silver at sixty cents per ounce, or slightly above the average price in the twenties.[16]

The preliminary conversations improved the white metal's prospects. While Pittman met with foreign delegates one May afternoon, the president talked with Senator King. The latter emerged to inform waiting newsmen that "you may be sure silver is going to find an improved status as a result of the [London] conference."[17]

The Economic Conference failed to cope with the world depression. It began on June 12 amid hopes of international cooperation reviving trade and easing the severe monetary stringency confronting many nations. The discussions quickly reached a stalemate, however, between the countries led by France, insisting upon currency stabilization, and others led by the United States seeking to stabilize domestic prices after appropriate increases.[18] Early in July, Roosevelt rebuked the delegates, deploring their "singular lack of proportion" and minimizing the importance of currency stabilization. He told the conference that the United States sought "the kind of a dollar which a generation hence will have the same purchasing and debt-paying power as the dollar value we hope to attain in the near future." That objective meant more than temporary stabilization of currencies. This message led to a "petulant outcry" that he had wrecked the conference.[19] Thereafter, the unhappy delegates remained in London for three additional weeks, but without significant accomplishment.

The Economic Conference had another unfortunate aspect. The American delegation had been casually selected, had no direction, and was given to quarreling in public over programs, procedures, and personalities.[20] Key Pittman, in particular, received criticism for his personal lapses. Herbert Feis, who also attended the conference, later recalled Pittman as being a "mean," narrow man interested only in silver and having little or no regard for foreign countries.[21] In discussing the senator's problem

79

with alcohol, Raymond Moley has said that most of the stories about Pittman's conduct at the conference were to his "personal knowledge gross exaggerations or untruths." He also noted that the "atmosphere of politics is always heavily laden with the fumes of alcohol," and that most participants live under constant strain. Moley, who was a good friend of the senator, said:

> In Pittman's case we have a brilliant mind coupled with a highly sensitive nervous system. Over the years alcoholic indulgence on a moderate scale ended in a case of genuine alcoholism. . . . If half the stories about the [London Conference] affair had been true, Pittman . . . would have been committed to protective custody.[22]

The senator from Nevada alone achieved a specific goal while in London, thereby saving the conference from total failure before it adjourned late that July. A presidential silver memorandum guided Pittman's actions. It instructed the American delegation to seek agreement by governments represented at London (1) to limit their sales of silver, (2) to refrain from debasing their coinage, (3) to restore their coinage to former grades of metallic purity, and (4) to establish an optional 20 percent silver reserve as backing for currency.[23]

Pittman also sought additional steps to ease the silver problem. He chaired the subcommittee on silver which reported to the Monetary and Financial Commission. Pittman's group first met on June 21; he soon became chairman of a smaller special committee dedicated to the task of negotiating an agreement on silver. The second group, composed of representatives from Mexico, Canada, Peru, Bolivia, India, China, and Spain, discussed "regulation of the supply of silver coming on the market from the mines" and limiting the flow from "government stocks." On July 5, the special committee announced that its sessions would be conducted in private and that it would report any progress.[24] Pittman gave daily luncheons for its members.[25] It was reported that his personal characteristics "improved the atmosphere for negotiations."[26]

Two of the delegates, T. V. Soong and Sir George Schuster,

became Pittman's allies early in the conference. "You were my most effective ally at the conference," the senator later wrote in reply to a friendly note from China's Soong. "I doubt seriously whether the resolutions would have been adopted or the agreement consummated except for your very able and active support." Apparently, Pittman continued to have cordial relations with this representative.[27] His other "effective ally," Sir George Schuster, finance member of the government of India, was responsible for management of India's currency affairs, including silver.[28] Schuster supported Pittman's aims throughout the conference.[29]

Negotiation of a workable silver agreement proceeded under persistent threat that the international conference might suddenly adjourn. Not until July 20 did the subcommittee on silver adopt a four-part resolution which began with the recommendation that "an agreement be sought between the chief silver producing countries and those countries which are the largest holders or users of silver with a view to mitigating fluctuations in the price of silver."[30] The delegates were also working on the proposed agreement, and two days later it was signed by representatives of the eight interested nations. In four more days, on July 26, supplemental accords were signed allocating purchase quotas among five producing nations, with the United States assuming by far the largest commitment. The conference adjourned the following day.[31] "I was constantly fighting to keep the conference in session so that I could obtain the agreement," Pittman later wrote Francis H. Brownell.[32]

The Silver Agreement of July 22, 1933, regulated the international marketing of silver for the following four years. The eight signatory nations requested that each of the sixty-six nations represented at London refrain from debasing its silver coinage. The three large consumer and holder nations agreed as follows: India would not sell more than thirty-five million ounces per year commencing January 1, 1934; Spain would not sell over twenty million ounces during the four-year period; and China would not sell silver "resulting from demonetized coins" during that period. The producing nations—the United States, Mexico,

81

Canada, Peru, and Australia—agreed not to sell silver during the period of agreement and to withhold from the market an aggregate of thirty-five million ounces per year out of their total domestic production. The individual quotas were twenty-four million ounces for the United States, seven million ounces for Mexico, one and one-half million ounces for Canada, one million ounces for Peru, and one-half million ounces for Australia.[33]

Upon returning to Washington in August, Pittman found that the terms of the Silver Agreement had provoked both negative and positive reactions from the West. Some were very pleased. Three Idaho silvermen telegraphed Pittman their "sincere congratulations on the fine accomplishments you have achieved" in advancing the "silver cause."[34] Similar feelings were expressed by Irvin E. Rockwell, who said:

> Those SOB's down in Manhattan regard us as sons of W[ild] J[ack] A[sses] fit only to march in goosestep to their music (this is literally true) and but for you and YOU ALONE, giving due credit to the others for beating the drum, silver as such would still be regarded by them as good only for knives and forks and spoons.[35]

If some westerners swelled with gratitude, many reacted otherwise. The editors of the *Salt Lake Tribune* lamented that the agreement was "No Help for Silver." Moreover, they felt that it would be "more of an obstacle than an aid to the ultimate objective of the silver movement."[36] Wheeler wrote to the president about that negative reaction, informing him that "we do not have much faith that the agreement reached in London on silver will do much good."[37] Wheeler had expressed this opinion publicly as well. Shortly after the London Conference began, Wheeler informed newspaper reporters that the program advocated by Senator Pittman would be of little benefit because "he is still treating [silver] as a commodity and not even as a favored commodity."[38] Pittman tacitly conceded the validity of Wheeler's complaints. He told George Snyder that if the president ratified the Silver Agreement, "the value of silver mines will be more greatly benefited than the value of silver."[39]

Wheeler's contentions, then, rather than Pittman's, reflected the discontentment reemerging in the West. The limited program agreed upon at London could not offset the disenchantment over generally declining commodity prices after midyear. Moreover, inflationists complained because the president failed to use his powers under the Thomas amendment.

The president sympathized with their point of view. His concern and his political instincts overcame both his own uncertainty and the resistance of his advisors in the Treasury Department. That fall he ordered a gold purchase program in order (1) to reduce the purchasing power of the dollar by a *de facto* devaluation and (2) to raise general commodity prices through reduction in the gold value of the dollar.[40] This would be accomplished, he hoped, by increasing the price paid for gold.[41] The program initiated a series of highly controversial monetary actions.

Before the president announced his new policy on gold, Pittman had been confidently awaiting a silver purchase program. Initially, he had taken a straightforward approach to winning Roosevelt's approval. On September 15, the senator submitted a four-page brief describing the poor condition of the mining industry in Nevada and Utah. He noted that the Thomas amendment gave the president authority to change this situation. Continuing, Pittman stressed that a profitable price for silver would stimulate general activity and employment since it was a by-product in most mining operations.[42] On September 19, he talked with the president about this and other subjects for more than two hours. Apparently Roosevelt disarmed the senator. In early October he wrote W. Mont. Ferry that "the President prefers to deal with only the American production of silver at the present time."[43] His optimism was premature.

Pittman's satisfaction vanished when Roosevelt failed even to mention silver in his "fireside chat" about the purpose of buying gold. Pittman claimed in a letter to the president the following day that raising the price of silver would do more to raise commodity prices than buying gold at a high price. In a reminder of his potent role in the field of foreign relations, Pittman also asserted that those who warned of some hardship to China due to

83

higher silver prices should be disregarded since that nation's minister of finance, T. V. Soong, had written that he was "happy" with the Silver Agreement. Finally, the senator employed the most forceful of his political arguments. After mentioning the rising clamor for inflation, Pittman suggested that "the possibility of [mandatory] legislation at the next session of Congress," returning the nation to the free coinage of silver at sixteen to one, made a good case for the president to act beforehand.[44]

Pittman solicited support from the president's assistant and political advisor, Louis McHenry Howe. This tactic was appropriate for two reasons: the senator's personal relations with Howe were cordial, and the latter was concerned about the discontent from the West. Pittman informed Howe about "the numerous letters and telegrams I am receiving from the West expressing disappointment that [the president] did not take up the silver problem."[45]

Pittman later elaborated to Howe these dangers for the president because "I know that the President relies upon you to relieve him . . . and to keep your eye upon the political situation." The senator warned that Roosevelt should take action because "our friend Bert Wheeler is about to start a riot among the silver producers of the West." Pittman saw the possibility of a movement "which might result in the necessity of the President vetoing an act of Congress relating thereto."[46]

Pittman tried to convince Howe that Roosevelt should disregard the objections to buying silver raised by professional economists. Howe shared the senator's disdain for the academicians' advice to the president. Pittman was dogmatic on this matter.

> I must contend that the general economists know little about the silver problem. They have studied under those who did not regard silver as money. . . . They have lived, spoken and lectured in such an environment. They are conservative by nature and are opposed to any unusual move. The President has gone far ahead of them. . . .[47]

The effect of Pittman's cultivation of Howe had limited value. The latter provided a conduit and a source of information for the senator but probably no more than that. Howe's biographer has emphasized that the influence his subject once had on Roosevelt waned sharply after the election, while that of his highly educated advisors grew.[48]

Pittman also sought help from a comparatively obscure member of the New Deal, Herman Oliphant, a little-known but respected legal expert. Prior to his governmental appointment, Oliphant had been professor of law at Johns Hopkins, and had also taught at Columbia and the University of Chicago. He filled a bill of particulars reportedly drafted by Roosevelt to guide those seeking a general counsel for the Farm Credit Administration. They wanted an attorney who had been brought up on a farm, "had not been in a Wall Street office, had a broad social viewpoint, was an outstanding lawyer and highly respected at the Bar."[49]

Oliphant's obscurity in Washington in no way diminished his aid to Key Pittman. Fortunately for the senator, Roosevelt named Oliphant the general counsel at the Treasury Department to assist Henry Morgenthau, Jr., who, on November 17, 1933, succeeded the ailing William Woodin.[50] In the two weeks preceding that realignment, Oliphant and Pittman became friends and learned to work together. The former Indiana farm boy and the silverite from Nevada agreed on the need for higher agricultural prices and monetary experimentation to that end. Their common views greatly helped the silver movement in the following months.

Pittman lauded Oliphant to the president. The day after their first working session the senator told Oliphant a letter was on its way to the White House saying that Oliphant "had the best grasp, not only of the legal situation involved but of the practical side of the problem of anyone connected with the Government with whom I have had the opportunity to confer."[51] Pittman put his high praise in writing, he admitted to Oliphant, because of his "hope that Mr. Morgenthau will bring you in contact with the President at an early date."[52]

Pittman provided Oliphant with answers to specific questions which he felt might be asked in conversations with Roosevelt. The most important item was the price of silver. Apparently the sena-

85

tor learned that Roosevelt had previously asked Secretary Woodin to "give serious consideration to some method of raising the price of silver to sixty cents an ounce."[53] Pittman was not entirely satisfied with this proposal. He told Oliphant that if the president seemed determined to fix the price somewhere near that figure, "it would simplify matters by simply taking half of the bullion for seigniorage, which would make the price sixty-four and one half cents an ounce."[54]

Pittman's seigniorage plan for establishing the Treasury's price used a frequently misunderstood monetary technique. He proposed that a 50 percent tax be assessed on all purchases of domestically mined silver. Producers would be paid the statutory price for silver, $1.29 per ounce. However, one half of the silver presented to the Treasury would become federal property by right of seigniorage. This would reduce the effective price to sixty-four and one half cents per ounce. While this price would give silver producers a handsome subsidy by 1933 prices, it only moderately exceeded the approximately fifty-nine cents per ounce average price during the twenties. Prices had declined from about eighty cents per ounce in 1920 to under forty cents per ounce ten years later.[55]

The senator must have known that his seigniorage plan would antagonize the bimetallists. These individuals were demanding free silver coinage, or the coinage without a seigniorage charge by the government. Bimetallists objected strongly when the Treasury acquired silver bullion at less than the statutory price of $1.29 per ounce. They were unimpressed by the dual role of silver as a money and a commodity. The statutory price assured them that silver was "basic money," but its fluctuating market price underscored its nature as a commodity. A comment by Senator Borah emphasized this ambiguity.

I do not think it is a sound proposition to undertake to peg the price of silver as a commodity. What I should like to see is the restoration of silver to its proper place in our monetary system—a primary money. Of course, out of this primary money is made a commodity. But we do not stop with it as a commodity, we provide for its use as money.[56]

While Pittman and Oliphant were useful sources of information, the president found other channels. One alternate source was Democrat Elbert D. Thomas of Utah. Senator-elect Thomas advocated a silver purchase program closely similar to that fashioned by the administration. In April, following the defeat of the Wheeler amendment, Thomas had met with Roosevelt to discuss his proposal. In May, he carefully outlined his plan in a letter, and in September Thomas telegraphed the president to remind him of that suggestion.[57]

The senator requested a simple and a limited program. He asked for the coinage of all silver offered to the Treasury derived from new American production. The only charge to the producers would be the customary nominal seigniorage to cover minting expense. Thomas believed his plan justifiable because the coined silver would be returned to the owner "to be used for wages, salaries and the cost of mining," and thus be put immediately into circulation. This plan, Thomas conceded, would not solve unemployment throughout the country, but it would restore scores of counties in six or seven states to normal conditions.[58]

The president asked about the legality of buying silver. Pittman said that the Thomas amendment to the Agricultural Adjustment Act, which contained grants of discretionary monetary authority, established Roosevelt's power to accept the white metal in exchange for silver certificates. Moreover, the senator asserted that since the Silver Agreement reached at London was only an understanding between delegates, it did not require ratification by the Senate.[59] The president did not contest Pittman's views, especially since Oliphant agreed with him. The Treasury's general counsel held that since the Thomas amendment granted the necessary authority, it would be "both unnecessary and unwise" to raise the general question of the president's power to purchase silver.[60]

It became apparent after mid-November that the president was delaying the proclamation of a silver program for political reasons. However, Pittman was increasingly confident. He told

87

Josephus Daniels, American Ambassador to Mexico, that the president would soon take action on silver and that it would "undoubtedly" be a step in the right direction. "We cannot go too far at once."[61] Pittman tempered his optimism with realism because he understood the president's role. During that year and for some time afterward, Roosevelt sought to contrive a balance of sectional forces through "broker leadership," to use the term favored by Professor Burns.[62] For obvious reasons, Pittman supported the president in his role as political broker. Roosevelt was right, Pittman told him, and he was winning his battle against depression and deflation.[63]

On December 21, 1933, the president proclaimed American acceptance of the Silver Agreement arranged at London. Using the suggestions of both Pittman and Thomas as to the quantity and the price, he ordered the Treasury Department to begin immediately to purchase and coin all silver "mined . . . from natural deposits in the United States" after that date. The seigniorage charge was 50 percent, resulting in an effective price of sixty-four and one half cents per ounce for silver presented to the mints. This program would continue until December 31, 1937, as specified in the Silver Agreement.[64]

The president's order to purchase all newly-mined American silver immediately stimulated production and employment. By offering a temporary subsidy for domestic silver, the president apparently hoped to reinvigorate a declining industry. Mineowners and operators knew that if they expanded existing operations and opened closed mines at least one of the metals they produced would be profitable during the following four years. The copper, lead, and zinc produced in combination with silver were not profitable at 1933 prices. Despite this, the mining industry responded enthusiastically and thousands of men returned to work.[65]

Reaction to the proclamation ranged from joy to gloom. The divergent western response paralleled earlier reaction to the Silver Agreement. On December 22, 1933, the *Denver Post* and the *Rocky Mountain News* published contrasting reactions; the *News* was ecstatic and the *Post* restrained. The editors of the latter believed Roosevelt had taken a step in the right direction, but only a step, advocating remonetization next. The editors of the *News*, however, specified that they were "satisfied to see silver treated as a commodity."[66] Senator Borah's comment illustrated the dissatisfaction felt by many silverites.

> Some of us have been greatly interested and—if it is not regarded as "Lese Majesty"—I would say amused at the President's silver gesture. My telegrams from those who ought to have been most pleased are all dissatisfied with the move. It may bring some additional price to silver as a commodity. But it is not even a beginning of the solution of the silver question.[67]

Irvin E. Rockwell told Borah that "truly, we asked for a fish and got a serpent."[68] Pittman expressed a quite different reaction. In writing to one of Borah's constituents, he exulted over Roosevelt's acceptance of his views rather than those of academic advisors, "particularly as to the price and as to having it unlimited as to quantity."[69]

Not all westerners conceded that this matter was materially important to their section. A *Rocky Mountain News* editorial suggested that the primary effect of the silver policy was psychological and political, not economic. "We rather doubt that silver as a commodity is important enough even in the economic life of our seven silver producing states to be a determining factor in prosperity."[70]

The most significant reaction to Roosevelt's new silver policy was not that of the West but that of the East. "Out West" the president's proclamation appeared at least well-intentioned; however, eastern reaction chose the opposite tack. Objections to federal favoritism for a western industry—the common view of silver purchases by the government—were exceeded only by outbursts denouncing Roosevelt's penchant toward monetary experimentation. The latter critics dwelled on the president's theoretical heresy and usually failed to mention that while the total money supply would be increased, the inflationary stimulus due to such coinage would be imperceptible.

Editorial comment in the eastern press tended to be highly critical. These editorialists impugned the monetary aspect of the silver policy, portraying it as a bribe to wean the Silver Bloc away from the agrarian inflationists in the Senate. An excellent example of this attitude appeared in the *Boston Post* saying, in part, that:

President Roosevelt seems to have made a very shrewd move in inaugurating his silver purchase policy on the eve of the coming session of Congress. The members from the silver States are pronounced inflationists, but particuarly because they think it would help silver. Now he has pleased the silver enthusiasts, the President can expect their help in fighting off demands of the more extreme inflationists.[71]

Other editorials were more critical in tone. The *New York Times* was disdainful of "The Silver-Purchase Plan," calling it an "uneconomic experiment, in substance a political 'sop' to the silver-mining states." Almost as biting was editorial comment in the *Boston Evening Transcript* that "as a currency measure, the latest decision at Washington seems largely in the nature of a political gesture to help keep the whip-hand of action centered at the White House."[72] Perhaps the most somber view was that found in the *Philadelphia Herald-Inquirer*. Its editors deplored "The Dollar in Politics," claiming that "the [silver purchase] step is of grave and ominous import, as the riotous cheers from Tonopah and Leadville bear witness." Finally, the editors of the *New York Herald-Tribune* objected that "the country is being habituated to the notion that the dollar belongs to the politicians."[73]

During this antisilver outburst, the few favorable comments appearing in the eastern press were written by noted columnists. Two writers, who attempted to explain both the objectives and the politics involved, were Walter Lippmann and David Lawrence. In a lengthy piece titled "The Silver Question," Lippmann reminded his readers that "it is very difficult for Americans of this generation to think dispassionately about silver. To a large part of the nation, the city dwellers, it is the symbol of dangers that were averted once and for all in 1896." He also explained that the silver issue had been dormant since 1896, but not dead.

Lippmann asserted that the fundamental merit in the case for more silver money derived from his belief that the recent collapse of world prices resulted in large measure from "an abnormal demand for gold" after 1925. In the new silver policy, Lippmann said, the president was experimenting with silver because he desired first "to raise the world price of silver in order to induce Asia to stop bidding for gold, and second, to use silver as a substitute for part of the gold reserve."[74]

Lawrence also adopted a positive and hopeful attitude. He believed that the silver purchase program was a "step forward" and a possible stimulus for American "trade with the Orient." He also discussed the political effects of the policy, noting his belief that the president had "brought to his side a group of western senators who might have proved strong allies to the Thomas inflation group."[75]

President Roosevelt ordered a silver purchase program over the objections of Borah and Wheeler and in response to the political realism espoused by Pittman. The latter emphatically rejected his colleagues' view. He plaintively asked a Utah producer:

Will we of the silver mining states ever realize that the advocacy of the free and unlimited coinage of silver by the United States of any silver that came from anywhere in the world put back the cause of silver for over 40 years? Will we still have the same hallucinations, based on the same arguments, fighting against the same majority? God knows that, if I did not have more interest in the welfare of our country, in its export trade, in its economic system, than some of our best friends in this country, I would drop the whole proposition.[76]

The president's proclamation rewarded several years of activity by the Silver Bloc. In the twenties, its response to lower prices for the white metal had been to seek purchases by the Treasury Department and to encourage the producers to develop export markets. By the early thirties, some members of the Bloc believed that genuine relief demanded an international agreement to increase its monetary use. Others advocated action by the United States to remonetize the metal, and several thought that the war

91

debts might be collected through increased use of the metal. Finally, some people proposed purchases by the Treasury similar to those suggested by the Bland-Allison Act and the Sherman Silver Purchase Act of the previous century; Roosevelt accepted the idea of a direct subsidy to the mining industry in a period of depression.

The government's purchase of silver from domestic producers eased their burdens but did not appreciably increase prices on the world market. This fact, and the continuing belief of many Americans that an increase in silver prices boded well for all commodity prices, pointed the direction of subsequent agitation to "do something for silver."

1. Interview with Burton K. Wheeler, September 17, 1962.
2. Pittman to Bourne, February 16, 1933, Pittman Papers, box 140, "B" folder.
3. *Salt Lake Tribune*, April 5, 1933; *Rocky Mountain News* (Denver), April 4, 6, 1933.
4. Moley has stressed Pittman's personal popularity in assessing his usefulness to Roosevelt. Moley, *First New Deal*, p. 369.
5. U.S., *Congressional Record*, 73d Cong., 1st Sess., 1933, LXXVII, Part 1 (March 9, 1933), 117. Other silver bills were offered by senators Bankhead of Alabama (S. 818, p. 859), Dill of Washington (S. 234, p. 194) and Wheeler of Montana (S. 70, p. 115). Bankhead and Dill proposed liberal silver purchase programs, and Wheeler wanted silver remonetization.
6. Moley, *First New Deal*, pp. 23–25.
7. U.S., Congress, Senate, *Silver and the Foreign Debt Payments*, 73d Cong., 1st Sess., 1933, Document No. 8, p. III.
8. U.S., *Congressional Record*, 73d Cong., 1st Sess., 1933, LXXVII, Part 3 (April 28, 1933), 2549–50. The Senate approved Hayden's amendment doubling (to $200,000,000) the amount of silver to be accepted.
9. U.S., Department of the Treasury, *Annual Report of the Secretary of the Treasury on the State of Finances . . . 1933*, 1933, Document No. 3058, p. 27. The Treasury received 22, 734,824 ounces which it valued at $11,367,412.
10. *Denver Post*, June 15, 1933.
11. U.S., *Foreign Relations . . . 1932*, I, 808–810; Hoover, *Memoirs*, III, 130; Israel, p. 89; Pittman to George W. Snyder, November 8, 1933, Pittman Papers, box 144, "S" folder.
12. U.S., Department of State, *Foreign Relations of the United States: Diplomatic Papers, 1933*, I, 680. Moley later said that he meant to say "intelligently" rather than "intellectually." Schlesinger, *Coming of the New Deal*, p. 230. The other delegates were the chairman, Cordell Hull, the secretary of State and a former senator from Tennessee; James M. Cox, former governor of Ohio and the Democratic candidate for the presidency in 1920; Senator James M. Couzens of Michigan; Samuel D. McReynolds of Tennessee, chairman of

the House Foreign Affairs Committee; and Ralph W. Morrison of Texas, a retired banker. U.S., *Foreign Relations . . . 1933*, I, 620, n. 32.

13. U.S., *Foreign Relations . . . 1933*, I, 516–26. See pp. 516–21 for talks with Canadian and Mexican delegates. The delicate question of India and silver was discussed with British officials in private, unofficial sessions.

14. *Ibid.*, pp. 521–26. 15. *New York Times*, June 15, 1933.

16. *Denver Post*, May 18, 1933. 17. *New York Times*, May 14, 1933.

18. Schlesinger, *Coming of the New Deal*, p. 214.

19. Samuel I. Rosenman (ed.), *The Public Papers and Addresses of Franklin D. Roosevelt*, II, *The Year of Crisis, 1933* (New York: Random House, 1938), 264–67.

20. The story of this conference is reported at length in three reminiscences: See Feis, *1933*, pp. 169–258; Warburg, *Long Road Home*, pp. 126–38; and Moley, *First New Deal*, pp. 420–96.

21. Feis, *1933*, p. 173.

22. Moley, *First New Deal*, p. 370. For a detailed account of Pittman's misconduct, see Feis, *1933*, pp. 189, 194–95, 256.

23. U.S., *Foreign Relations . . . 1933*, I, 626. Memorandum on policy for the American delegation, May 30, 1933. The writer has paraphrased and interpreted the memorandum to suggest its intent.

24. League of Nations, *Journal of the Monetary and Economic Conference, London, 1933* (Geneva, Switzerland: Documents Service for the Monetary and Economic Conference, June, 1933), No. 11 (June 22), 101; No. 15 (June 27), 101; No. 22 (July 5), 146.

25. Pittman to Brownell, August 30, 1933, Pittman Papers, box 140, "B" folder.

26. *New York Times*, July 21, 1933. Clarence K. Streit wrote the special report in London.

27. Pittman to Soong, September 28, 1933, Pittman Papers, box 144, "S" folder.

28. Leavens, *Silver Money*, p. 183. Between 1928 and 1934, he sold nearly 200,000,000 ounces of silver.

29. *New York Times*, June 26, 1933. Pittman later said that he had enjoyed working with Schuster. Pittman to Francis H. Brownell, August 30, 1933, Pittman Papers, box 140, "B" folder.

30. League of Nations, *Journal of the Monetary and Economic Conference, London, 1933*, No. 35 (July 28, 1933), 208–09.

31. U.S., *Statutes at Large*, XLVIII, 73d Cong., 1933–34, Part 2, Executive Agreement Series, No. 63, *Silver Agreement: Memorandum of Agreement Between the United States of America, Australia, Canada, China, India, Mexico, Peru, and Spain, with Supplementary Undertakings*, pp. 1879–88.

32. Pittman to Brownell, August 30, 1933, Pittman Papers, box 140, "B" folder.

33. U.S., *Statutes at Large*, XLVIII, Part 2, 1882–88.

34. Telegram, James P. McCarthy, H. G. Washburn, and Stanley A. Easton to Pittman, August 9, 1933, Pittman Papers, box 145, "Mc" folder. Each represented a different mining company.

35. Rockwell to Pittman, September 12, 1933, Pittman Papers, box 145, "R" folder.

36. *Salt Lake Tribune*, July 25, 1933.

37. Wheeler to Roosevelt, July 31, 1933, Franklin D. Roosevelt Papers (Franklin D. Roosevelt Library, Hyde Park, New York), PPF 723—James A. Farley. Hereafter cited as Roosevelt Papers.

38. *New York Times*, June 24, 1933. The following day Wheeler said that the adoption of the American resolutions on silver "would be the most backward step . . . since 1873." *New York Times*, June 25, 1933. Wheeler may have been piqued that Pittman had ignored his Senate resolution, which instructed the American delegates to promote bimetallism exclusively, despite its approval by that body. U.S., *Congressional Record*, 73d Cong., 1st Sess., 1933, LXXVII, Part 3 (May 8, 1933), 2967.

39. Pittman to Snyder, December 12, 1933, Pittman Papers, box 144, "S" folder.

40. Rosenman (ed.), *Public Papers*, II, 420–27. The date of this announcement was October 22, 1933.

41. Schlesinger, *Coming of the New Deal*, pp. 239–40; see also Chapter VI.

42. Pittman, "Emergency Mining Legislation," September 15, 1933, Pittman Papers, box 142, Government Departments folder.

43. Pittman to Ferry, October 13, 1933, Pittman Papers, box 142, "F" folder.

44. Pittman to Roosevelt, October 23, 1933, Pittman Papers, box 142, Government Departments folder.

45. Pittman to Howe, October 28, 1933, Pittman Papers, box 142, Governments Departments folder.

46. Pittman to Howe, November 1, 1933, Pittman Papers, box 142, Government Departments folder.

47. Pittman to Howe, October 28, 1933, Pittman Papers, box 142, Government Departments folder.

48. Alfred B. Rollins, Jr., *Roosevelt and Howe* (New York: Alfred A. Knopf, 1962), p. 8.

49. Allan Seymour Everest, *Morgenthau, The New Deal and Silver; A Story of Pressure Politics* (New York: King's Crown Press, 1950), pp. 34–35.

50. U.S., *Annual Report of the Secretary of the Treasury . . . 1934*, 1935, Document No. 3065, p. xiii.

51. Pittman to Oliphant, November 1, 1933, Pittman Papers, box 142, Government Departments folder.

52. Pittman to Oliphant, November 1, 1933, Pittman Papers, box 142, Government Departments folder. The same day, the senator wrote to Louis Howe that Oliphant had "a clearer grasp of the law affecting the silver problem and the practical approach to it than anyone. . . ." Presumably, Howe so informed the president.

53. Memorandum: The president to the secretary of the Treasury, September 20, 1933, Roosevelt Papers, POF 229, box 3.

54. Pittman to Oliphant, November 3, 1933, Pittman Papers, box 142, Government Departments folder.

55. G. Griffith Johnson, Jr., *The Treasury and Monetary Policy* (Cambridge, Massachusetts: Harvard University Press, 1939), p. 173; Leong, p. 104.

56. Borah to Frank E. Johnesse, December 8, 1933, Borah Papers, box 353, Silver folder.

57. *Denver Post*, January 29, 1933; Thomas to Roosevelt, May 20, 1933, Thomas to Roosevelt, September 10, 1933, Roosevelt Papers, POF 229, box 2.

58. Thomas to Roosevelt, May 20, 1933, Roosevelt Papers, POF 229, box 2.

59. Pittman to Morgenthau, December 11, 1933, Pittman Papers, box 142, Government Departments folder.

60. Oliphant to Pittman, November 3, 1933, Pittman Papers, box 142, Government Departments folder. Oliphant also told Pittman of a second legal

authority to purchase newly mined silver for monetary purposes: "The [Sherman Silver Purchase] Act conferred upon the Secretary of the Treasury the privilege, power and duty to buy silver. The express language of the later Acts go no further than to abrogate his duty, leaving his privilege and power intact, although this certainly has not been the common understanding of the subsequent legislation."

61. Pittman to Daniels, November 9, 1933, Pittman Papers, box 142, "D" folder.

62. James McGregor Burns, *Roosevelt: the Lion and the Fox* (New York: Harcourt, Brace and Company, 1956), p. 197.

63. Pittman to Roosevelt, November 15, 1933, Pittman Papers, box 142, Government Departments folder.

64. U.S., *Statutes at Large,* XLVIII, 73d Cong., 1933–34, Part 2, Proclamation No. 2067, *Coinage of Silver,* pp. 1723–25.

65. Israel, p. 95. Metal mining employment in the mountain states totaled 57,147 in 1920, declined sharply to 48,113 in 1930, but returned to 52,836 by 1940. Arrington, *Changing Economic Structure,* pp. 35–37.

66. *Denver Post,* December 22, 1933; *Rocky Mountain News* (Denver), December 22, 1933.

67. Borah to Raymond Robbins, December 27, 1933, Borah Papers, box 352, Col. Raymond Robbins folder.

68. Rockwell to Borah, January 6, 1934, Borah Collection, Rockwell file.

69. Pittman to Ray H. Kingsbury, January 4, 1934, Pittman Papers, box 144, "K" folder.

70. *Rocky Mountain News* (Denver), December 23, 1933. Editorial, "The Silver Policy."

71. *Boston Post,* December 22, 1933.

72. *New York Times,* December 23, 1933; *Boston Evening Transcript,* December 22, 1933.

73. *Philadelphia Herald-Inquirer,* December 22, 1933; *New York Herald-Tribune,* December 23, 1933. The *Herald-Inquirer's* editors attributed the silver purchase scheme to a highly organized lobby in Washington.

74. *New York Herald-Tribune,* December 27, 1933. Lippmann endorsed experiment, but he was uncertain about the role of silver in the monetary system.

75. *Denver Post,* December 25, 1933.

76. Pittman to George W. Snyder, November 8, 1933, Pittman Papers, box 144, "S" folder.

6 Gold, Silver, and Inflation

In the fall of 1933, demands resounded in the countryside for remonetizing silver and raising commodity prices. The latter had risen that spring and early summer, but reversed thereafter triggering a renewal of agitation.[1] Senator Burton K. Wheeler resumed his campaign to restore the white metal, and Elmer Thomas began pleading for more money for circulation and a decrease in the dollar's purchasing power. The latter also worked closely with Father Charles E. Coughlin to support the president's monetary experiments and to urge him to even bolder efforts in that field. Thomas' goal was a dollar worth much less in terms of gold and thus a direct stimulus to higher prices for commodities.

Congressional inflationists such as Thomas and Wheeler had been quiet for several months after adoption of the Agricultural Adjustment Act in May. That law had assured federal assistance to the nation's farmers by providing new powers for the secretary of Agriculture and by granting the president authority to expand the currency, including the remonetization of silver, through the Thomas amendment. By September, however, western and southern legislators began complaining to Roosevelt, entreating him to increase the supply of money as a means of raising commodity prices.[2]

Thomas was the most outspoken senator participating in the agitation. He had advocated currency manipulation since his boyhood on a farm in Indiana. His preoccupation with the issue had been intense when he participated in collegiate debates during the late nineties. He retained a strong interest in the money ques-

97

tion throughout his career as lawyer and state legislator in Oklahoma, as a congressman in Washington after 1922, and as a senator after 1926.[3] Later, he even prepared a handbook on monetary management titled *Financial Engineering*.[4] Thomas' strong interest in this subject and his friendship with Senator Ellison D. "Cotton Ed" Smith of South Carolina, chairman of the Committee on Agriculture, made him the link between the Farm Bloc and the Silver Bloc.[5] His inflationary measure of April, 1933, was a classic example of fusion of interests. Thomas later said that in all of his agitation for monetary inflation his goal was "the best method to attain the end desired—higher prices."[6]

Thomas was proud of his amendment to the farm bill and he defended it against attacks by opponents of inflation. One of these was Fred I. Kent, foreign exchange controller for the Federal Reserve Bank of New York, who had both a professional interest in avoiding monetary fluctuations and a strong commitment to the status quo. In an article published in July, 1933, entitled "The Mystery of the Gold Standard," Kent explained the benefits to the nation resulting from a precise measure of the value of the dollar. He deplored the recent abandonment of the gold standard by the United States and urged its prompt restoration as a prerequisite to a revival of world trade and domestic recovery. Moreover, he declared that the Thomas amendment was "immoral," and charged that it had been forced through the Congress and into the statutes by unprincipled "forces of disruption."[7] In response, Thomas informed Kent that those forces to which he so strongly objected still existed because "the money question—the control of the value of the dollar—is the most important issue in the government." That question had been obscured for decades, Thomas said, but it had finally come into the open and it would remain there until satisfaction was achieved by "the producing masses" of the country.[8]

Thomas obtained support for his demands from the conference of cotton growers held in Washington that September. It had endorsed his resolution urging the president to undertake monetary inflation utilizing "non-interest bearing Treasury notes," often called greenbacks. On September 19, 1933, Thomas and

Senator "Cotton Ed" Smith led a large delegation representing nine states that produced cotton to present that resolution at the White House. They intended to confront the president, but he was not available due to a sudden "indisposition." One of his secretaries, Stephen Early, sent them to see Henry A. Wallace, the secretary of Agriculture, who in the meantime had departed from his office for an important meeting elsewhere.[9]

The cotton producers' agitation for more money in circulation reflected unrest in rural areas. It was the first instance of an attempt by a discontented group to invade the White House during the New Deal, according to Oliver McKee, who reported the event for the *Boston Evening News*. He also noted that he would not be surprised if "the wheat and other farmers of the Middle West and the Northwest also were to invade Washington with inflationary demands."[10]

As agrarian discontent continued to increase, Thomas promised that if the administration failed to provide significant currency inflation by the following January, he would offer a resolution to make it mandatory.[11] The senator's demand for greenbacks underscored his dissatisfaction with the policies of the Federal Reserve Board. The governor of that board, Eugene R. Black, wrote to Thomas in a strong defense of its operations, and the senator replied with equal vigor. Thomas offered several specific criticisms of these policies and then explained why he was insisting that the Federal Reserve banks must share their exclusive powers of issuance with the Treasury Department.

> Under normal conditions, I would not propose direct issue of non-interest bearing Treasury notes. . . . I recognize that it is natural for bankers in charge of the Federal Reserve System to be jealous of any proposal for the Treasury to issue its currency instead of leaving that privilege exclusively in the Federal Reserve. However, the gold-laden Federal Reserve cannot accomplish depreciation of the dollar from its gold parity by issuing its own notes. Therefore, this result must be attained through direct Treasury issuance. The Federal Reserve should not, and I hope will not, stand in the way.[12]

Thomas advocated in addition to greenbacks an assortment of inflationary devices. That fall, he presented a paper entitled "Money and Its Management" to a session of the American Academy of Political and Social Science meeting in Philadelphia. His comments, concise and well written, included ideas and phrases that often appeared in his correspondence on the money question. Thomas outlined a program for increasing the supply of money in actual circulation involving (1) purchases of gold in order to devalue the paper dollar; (2) purchases of silver intended to increase its price followed by a wider use of silver in the monetary system; (3) expansion of public works; (4) devaluation of the gold dollar and a return to the gold standard thereafter; and (5) the circulation of monetary gold after revaluation. Implicitly, Thomas rejected the admonition of Wesley C. Mitchell, an eminent economist, who earlier had told him that "the reason why prices do not rise at present is, I think, not that there is any inadequacy in the circulating medium, but rather that there is so little prospect of profit in using the money now available."[13]

The senator's proposals and arguments for monetary reform and inflation led his critics to claim that he used a ghost writer, George L. Le Blanc. The latter was Thomas' friend and a prominent but unorthodox investment counselor who formerly was vice-president in charge of the foreign department at the New York Equitable Trust. Le Blanc "helps the good Senator write . . . his letters and speeches," said James P. Warburg after he became an articulate opponent of the president's monetary experiments and inflation.[14] Le Blanc replied immediately: "It is only fair to the Senator for me to state emphatically that I have never written any of Thomas' speeches or letters, although I have been consulted in statements of fact which he has used."[15] Although Thomas may have had some other assistance, there was evidence to support Le Blanc's rebuttal. Long before Warburg's accusation, Le Blanc had written Thomas to congratulate him on the contents of a letter to Eugene R. Black. "I have a copy of your letter to Governor Black on the money question. . . . I congratulate you regarding the clear way of pointing out the present danger and a remedy to avoid it: it is close to perfection."[16]

Another avowed inflationist with whom Thomas became associated that fall was Father Charles E. Coughlin, the radio-priest from Michigan. The widespread public response to his Sunday afternoon broadcasts was largely a reaction to the depression and the uncertainties it brought to many Americans.[17] His popularity as a crusader for the people was then reaching its highest level. He reported to the president that he had received 600,000 letters during the first two weeks of November.[18] These expressed concern about such matters as "war bonds, . . . restoration of silver, . . . and nationalization of gold," Coughlin informed Stephen Early, adding that "I will be glad to send you a few truck loads."[19]

During October and November, 1933, the priest devoted his radio talks to a discussion of the money question. In the first of these discourses delivered to a vast listening audience, he said that the dollar had become a "flat tire," and he insisted that it must be reinflated "so that we can travel along the highway of . . . prosperity." In his third broadcast of that series, Coughlin urged the restoration of silver, assuring his listeners that "the Teapot Dome was nothing compared to the Demonetization Act" in 1873. He also charged that the prevalent low price for silver had "succeeded in putting China and India on the loin cloth standard of living."[20] To remedy the domestic situation, Coughlin urged the adoption of "a new dollar, a new American dollar, which contains approximately 25 cents in gold and 75 cents in silver. This is a perfectly conservative estimate of the value of silver—75 cents an ounce. . . . Today it is 42 cents an ounce."[21]

The power of Father Coughlin's advocacy was such that Senator Thomas could not afford to reject the priest's vague plan for changing the monetary value of silver. Previously he had invited Coughlin to present his monetary ideas at a Washington conference in mid-November sponsored by the Committee for the Nation to Rebuild Prices and Purchasing Power. Coughlin was unable to attend, however, and he asked the senator to present the remonetization plan, directing him to be very specific about the new dollar having "75 cents silver and 25 cents gold."[22] Thomas complied with Coughlin's request despite his knowledge that the Silver Bloc would never consent to reduce the statutory

101

price for monetary silver from $1.29 per ounce to seventy-five cents. The other senators at the gathering included Smith of South Carolina and Bryan Patton Harrison of Mississippi, chairman of the Committee on Finance and an advocate of immediate inflationary action by the president.[23] Borah, Wheeler, and Pittman had been invited but they failed to attend, although Pittman sent his regrets and a lengthy statement of position on silver and the money question.[24] Undeterred by the lack of representation from the Silver Bloc, the conferees endorsed Coughlin's plan to fix the monetary value of silver at seventy-five cents per ounce.[25]

While Thomas and Coughlin agitated for inflation, others attacked the president for initiating such measures. Opponents of monetary manipulation protested his buying gold as a means to devalue the dollar, raise commodity prices, and pacify the agrarian unrest so prevalent at that time.[26] Shortly after starting that controversial experiment in October, moreover, Roosevelt appointed his old friend, Henry Morgenthau, Jr., secretary of the Treasury despite his lack of financial experience.

Four days later, on November 21, 1933, Professor O. M. W. Sprague resigned from his advisory post with the Treasury in protest over the new paths in monetary policy and Morgenthau's appointment. The same day, an article titled "The Dangers of Inflation" by Bernard M. Baruch, a prominent financier, advisor to presidents, and a Democrat, was published in a popular weekly magazine, the *Saturday Evening Post*. The author warned his readers that inflated currency was "an enemy of mankind and an act of desperation." He offered many arguments against such action and he urged opposition to the threat posed by "the tyranny of an inflamed majority."[27] The editors of the *New York Times* commended Baruch's sober appraisal of the issue.[28]

Alfred E. Smith, former governor of New York, Democratic candidate for the presidency in 1928, and political mentor of the president, was the national figure most vigorous in his rejection of Roosevelt's monetary policies.[29] When the latter deliberately began to experiment with money, Smith scornfully remarked that "I am for gold dollars and against baloney dollars." As to the proper policy, Smith recommended that Roosevelt should oppose innovation and inflation as Cleveland had done in the nineties.

What the people need today is what the Bible centuries ago described as "the shadow of a great rock in a weary land." That was what Grover Cleveland represented to the people in his day—a symbol of strength and firmness, of coolness, of rock-like integrity in the midst of shifting sands, heat and desolation. . . . I am for a return to the gold standard.[30]

The nation's leading economists also repudiated the president's monetary policies. Professor Sprague warned of possible unrestrained inflation and the complete breakdown of the government's credit. Forty economists led by Professor Edwin W. Kemmerer of Princeton organized the Economists' National Committee on Monetary Policy "to refute soft-money heresies."[31] This group correctly predicted that monetary experiment would not cause commodity prices to rise appreciably, but it grossly exaggerated the potential harm to the nation. Its warnings and often conflicting technical arguments exasperated individuals like General Hugh S. Johnson, head of the National Recovery Administration, who castigated the entire discipline as "a tangle of conjecture, about which no two or three solemn pundits agree." He also said that their talk about impairment of federal credit was inappropriate because the United States was a creditor nation with a favorable balance of trade and possessed 40 percent of the world's supply of monetized gold.[32]

The controversy over money seemed to have political implications for the future. The *New York Times* reported strong bipartisan support for the president in the West, the South, and also in many eastern communities. Senator George K. Norris predicted a realignment of parties on the money question that would become evident in the following session of the Congress. He also anticipated that the issue would dominate the congressional election campaign that fall.[33]

Political overtones were obvious late that November when Thomas and Coughlin appeared at a rally organized to demonstrate support for the president's inflationary policies and to rebuke his opponents. At the Hippodrome in New York City, an enthusiastic crowd in excess of ten thousand persons applauded all references to Roosevelt and roundly berated his critics. These persons also cheered lustily each time the priest and the senator urged the president to take additional inflationary action.[34]

Early in December, Thomas praised the priest for the successful rally and assured him that the president would soon start expanding the currency. "I look forward to much activity . . .; otherwise, there will be really only one question before the Congress . . ., the immediate adjustment of the value of the dollar." Thomas asserted that Coughlin's straightforward rebuttal of "Al" Smith's attack on the president had silenced that opponent of inflation.[35]

The extreme views on the money question seemed to offset each other. One of the president's advisors, Senator James F. Byrnes of South Carolina, thought the argument had retarded inflationism in the Senate. He told Roosevelt that soft money advocates would "give us more trouble in the next session [of Congress] than the few who hold and express the [opposite] views." Louis Howe wrote, "I agree with this 100 percent" across the face of Byrnes' letter and the president added, "So do I, F.D.R."[36]

The controversy over inflation and monetary policy presented opportunities for silver advocates. In the midst of the arguments, one perceptive historian commented upon the president's need to secure majority approval for his proposals in the Congress and the feeling among "silver men . . . that somewhere in their territory lies the middle ground: the South with its paper and the East with its gold must lay down their arms before the West with its silver."[37]

Senator Thomas proposed an action relevant to the nation's stock of gold which subsequently led to another advance for the silver movement. He suggested that both title to and possession of monetary gold be transferred from Federal Reserve banks to the Treasury Department.[38] His objective was political control over the privately owned Federal Reserve system, and its loss of gold would be evidence to him of a transfer of power over money

WEATHER FORECAST
UTAH — Fair and
Sunday and Friday.
Partly Cloudy Thursday

IDAHO — Generally fair
Sunday and Friday.

The Salt Lake Tribune

LOCAL METAL PRICES
Gold $35.00
Silver (domestic) ...... 64¼¢
Silver (foreign) .... 45¢
Lead .... 3.90¢
Copper .... 9.00¢
Lead ... 4.25¢   Zinc ... 4.35¢
Lead ... 4.25¢   Copper ... 9.00¢

9, NO. 33.

SALT LAKE CITY, UTAH, THURSDAY MORNING, MAY 17, 1934.

24 PAGES—FIVE CENTS

SILVER AGREEMENT REACHED

HOPE GROWS FOR WORLD ARMS TRUCE

England, France Express Willingness to Make Concessions

Geneva Crisis Near

U. S., Other Powers May Join to End War in Gran Chaco

By Associated Press

Hopeful signs for world peace and disarmament, mingled with rumors of a forced crisis at Geneva placed a new face on the arms problem on Wednesday.

A proposal was in the air at Geneva to abandon the disarmament conference and report its failure to the league of nations, possibly in an attempt to force France to show her hand on the question of guarantees.

The French foreign minister made plain that his country is keeping an open door to further discussions, and the British foreign secretary declared England is ready to "make any reasonable concession" to bring about an agreement.

There were rumors that Germany is showing signs of willingness to return to the conference. In Norway the sterling crippled by a close vote in the league.

Falls to Death

E. B. Palmer

FORMER S. L. BANKER FOUND DEAD IN HILLS

Discovery of E. B. Palmer's Body Ends Week-long Search

The search for Eugene Boylan Palmer, widely known in Salt Lake as an investment banker and news-paper man, ended Wednesday when his body was found on the south bank of the Tuba river, four miles from Washington, Nevada county, California.

NEW DEAL FOES HAIL REED VOTE

Republicans See Renomi-nation as Sentiment Against Administration

DEMOCRATS DIFFER

Declare G. O. P. Victory in G. O. P. State Nothing of Significance

By Associated Press

WASHINGTON, May 16—Republicans declarations that the renomination of Senator Reed of Pennsylvania, sharp-tongued foe of the Roosevelt program, mirrored sentiment against the administration policies clashed today with blunt Democratic counter assertions.

Achieve Accord for White Metal Legislation

ROOSEVELT SET TO ASK FOR ACTION

Special Message to Urge Two-Point Pro-gram on Congress

Senators Are Jubilant

Mandatory Purchase Provided to Set Up 25 Per Cent Reserve

By SAM BLEDSOE

WASHINGTON, May 16 — Silver legislation at this session was decided upon today after a two-hour conference between President Roosevelt and the senate silver bloc.

U. S. Indicts Abductors To Block Parole Chance

Kidnapers of Coast Millionaire Face Charges of Using Mails for Extortion

LOS ANGELES, May 16 (UP)—The government acted in mowie fashion today to block the possibility of parole for any of the kidnapers of William F. Gettle...

HICKMAN GIVES NEW VERSION

Silver Measure to Carry Administration Approval

Roosevelt and Pittman to Confer on Pur-chase Plan Before Drafting of Bill

By HARRY J. BROWN
Tribune Correspondent
WASHINGTON, May 16—President Roosevelt, at his conference with the silver bloc of the senate this afternoon...

Two Airmen Plan Distance Flight; Other Pair Will Continue to Rome

Will Rogers Says

Britain's Anthony Eden in
a private session with
Senator Key Pittman of
Nevada, silver bloc leader
and author of Pittman Act
that briefly curbed
the sinking price of silver.

The "Lion of Idaho,"
Senator William E. Borah,
was an outspoken
champion of silver.
Borah later became the
chief Republican spokesman
on U.S. foreign policy.

*Oklahoma Congressman
Elmer Thomas set off
bitter controversy when he
demanded "complete federal
control of the monetary
system and controlled
monetary inflation."*

*Montana Senator Burton K. Wheeler
was one of the big three of
the silver bloc in the 1930's.
Wheeler also joined with
Oklahoma's Elmer Thomas
in advocating monetary inflation.*

to Washington. This proposal complemented his continuing insistence upon devaluing the dollar. Subsequent adoption of these two schemes prepared the way for legislation requiring a major increase in silver stocks to augment the nation's monetary reserve.

The senator's demands for seizure of the Federal Reserve's gold were politically viable during this emotion-filled period. His plan reflected the prevalent distrust of bankers among the people and their leaders. Two of these, the president and the radio-priest, expressed this attitude in the fall of 1933. Father Coughlin supported the demands for Treasury control over all money because of "a great uprising in opinion against the questionable privilege extended to the national banks of printing their own money on the basis of 40 per cent gold deposit or value deposit." He held that this function should be reserved to the federal government.[39] The president, in a letter to Colonel House, expressed a similar view:

The real truth of the matter is, as you and I know, that a financial element in the larger centers has owned the Government ever since the days of Andrew Jackson—and I am not wholly excepting the Administration of Woodrow Wilson. The country is going through a repetition of Jackson's fight with the Bank of the United States—only on a far bigger and broader basis.[40]

The president incorporated the transfer of monetary gold in his program to revalue the dollar. In December, he ordered the Treasury to study a plan to raise its price from $20.67 to $35.00 per ounce, thereby devaluing and stabilizing the dollar in terms of that metal.[41] Treasury ownership and physical possession of all monetary gold correlated with the larger policy because it answered the question of how to account for the "profit" which would be created if the price of gold was increased in terms of dollars. He could have done this by a proclamation, using a power granted by the Thomas amendment, but he chose to request specific legislation to that end. Thomas' original excuse for demanding the physical transfer of gold stocks from vaults in the Federal Reserve banks to the Treasury in exchange for gold

105

certificates was based upon the problem of the "profit" from devaluation.[42]

The Federal Reserve Board strenuously objected to the actual transfer of its gold stocks. It proposed that a "bookkeeping transfer" between each of the banks and the Treasury would be simpler and just as effective.

Thomas disliked the board's rejoinder and attempted to prevent its consideration. Early in January, 1934, he sent a night letter to Father Coughlin informing him of the bankers' counteroffer and his own objections.

> FEDERAL RESERVE BANKS SAY THEY WILL COOPERATE TO GIVE TREASURY DEVALUATION PROFIT AS A CREDIT TRANSACTION BUT NOT NECESSARY TO TRANSFER BULLION. . . . I AM DEMANDING THAT FEDERAL RESERVE BANKS SURRENDER TO FEDERAL TREASURY SUCH GOLD.[43]

The priest immediately supported Thomas' demand for seizure of the Reserve System's gold. He also castigated the "bargaining" tactics of the bankers.[44] Meanwhile, Thomas gathered sufficient support from his senatorial colleagues to make a firm stand on the issue.[45]

Officials of the Federal Reserve System resisted the mounting pressure to surrender its supply of gold.[46] They correctly regarded the plan as a reduction of their powers and prerogatives. In his comments on the bankers' objections, Arthur Krock lamented that "in ordinary times . . . these proposals would not be taken seriously at all."[47] G. G. Johnson deprecated the strong reaction among banking officials to the proposals for a federal gold reserve.

> The indignation among financial interests over this rather academic point was probably greater than that aroused by any other provision of the Gold Reserve bill. The practical importance of the provision was small, but it probably resulted psychologically in a further impairment of the prestige of the Reserve System.[48]

106

On January 15, 1934, the president sent to Congress a message on gold. He asked that the government be empowered: to take title and possession of all monetary gold; to forbid the use of gold coin; to issue gold for settlement of international balances only; and to take the "profit" resulting from devaluation. The president also asked for authority to fix the devaluation at between 50 and 60 percent of the old parity, and to establish a two-billion dollar exchange equalization fund employing dollars created by the devaluation.[49] In effect, Roosevelt wanted a new departure in American policy; Britain already employed the latter technique with success.[50]

Congress approved the president's request virtually without alteration. The Gold Reserve Act gave the United States title to the Federal Reserve's gold and specified its physical transfer upon demand by the Treasury.

All gold so transferred . . . shall be held in custody for the United States and delivered upon the order of the Secretary of the Treasury . . . and the Federal Reserve Board . . ., Banks . . ., [and] agents shall give such instructions and shall take such action as may be necessary to assure that such gold shall be so held and delivered.[51]

Thomas did not offer his bill for sequestration as he had threatened to do if the administration failed to present its bill. Thomas' proposal read, in part:

Sec. 4. Within .... days after the date of enactment of this Act, each Federal Reserve Bank shall transfer and deliver to the control of the Treasurer of the United States to be held by him on behalf of the United States all gold coins and gold bullion owned by such bank and in exchange therefor, the Secretary of the Treasury is authorized and directed to issue to each such bank gold certificates in a face amount equal to the value of the gold coin or bullion so transferred and delivered. . . .[52]

Swift congressional approval emphasized the importance of the measure. To Professor John M. Blum, the significance of the act was that it "turned over to the Treasury much of the authority for the management of credit and currency," making monetary control an instrument of national policy.[53] G. G. Johnson held that it furthered the idea that "the value of the dollar in terms of gold and foreign exchange is a legitimate instrument for serving domestic political ends."[54]

An editorial in the *Commercial and Financial Chronicle* gave the business community's view of the new locus of monetary authority and power.

> The Reserve Authorities have been reduced to shadowy non-entities, the Federal Reserve System having become simply an adjunct to the Federal Government, to do what they are told to do. . . . The proposition as far as the Federal Reserve System is concerned is simply one of Stand and Deliver.[55]

Senator Thomas endorsed the New Deal policy on gold. After the president requested a Federal Gold Reserve, Thomas explained that since the government guaranteed all paper money it was proper that all monetary metal be in its vaults. He also observed that "all monetary silver likewise is to be nationalized, [although] subsidiary silver [coins] will continue to circulate and perhaps some silver dollars." Finally, he noted that "the exact status of silver in our monetary policy has not been fixed; hence it is a matter for future consideration and adjustment."[56]

The president acknowledged that he had not as yet established a permanent policy on silver as a monetary metal. Anticipating congressional disappointment with his message relating to gold, Roosevelt spoke kindly concerning the white metal.

> The other principal precious metal—silver—has also been used from time immemorial as a metallic base for currencies as well as for actual currency itself. It is used as such by probably half the population of the world. It constitutes a very important part of our own monetary structure. It is such a crucial factor in much of the world's international trade that it cannot be neglected.[57]

108

Then Roosevelt informed the Congress that he had issued a directive on December 21, 1933, to purchase and coin all newly mined American silver pursuant to the Silver Agreement negotiated at London. He further noted that the nations represented at the Monetary and Economic Conference had agreed not to impair further the monetary use and value of silver. The president also said that since the result of these actions would soon be very helpful, he had no additional measures to propose at that time.[58]

Western senators regretted the president's failure to request legislation on silver. Wheeler, Borah, and King agreed that the silver drive should be pressed forward even though Roosevelt preferred that they await future events. Adopting the obvious strategy, they decided to propose an amendment to the Gold Reserve bill when it reached the Senate floor.

The president, by proposing to revalue gold, made obsolete the historic ratio of sixteen to one, and by rejecting bimetallism in any form, crippled Senator Wheeler's campaign.[59] During November and December, the senator had mobilized support for remonetization. Just before the Congress reconvened in January, he published a list of twenty-seven senators who endorsed the goal. The list included Borah, who had dropped his insistence on the international approach. Wheeler compromised, however, favoring bimetallism: "the free and unlimited coinage of both gold and silver at a ratio to be established by law." He said that seventeen other senators, including Bronson Cutting of New Mexico, and Pittman, had expressed sympathy but did not endorse the statement.[60] Wheeler had forty-four votes at the most, not enough to win on a roll call.

Lacking the votes to carry mandatory bimetallism in principle even without a fixed ratio of silver to gold, Wheeler changed his course. He had been outmaneuvered by Roosevelt, who, in December, had ordered purchases of domestic silver, and in January had asked the Congress to devalue the dollar. Wheeler, after a brief tactical retreat to an unspecified ratio, eventually abandoned the principle of bimetallism. The other senators accepted that

109

decision with little if any criticism. Later, Wheeler recalled the events of that period.

I never thought many of the Senators from the West were [as] enthusiastic about the remonetization of silver as I was. Most of them I think felt as Roosevelt did that politically it was an unwise thing to do but most of the people who voted for it [did so because] they felt at that particular time [that] something had to be done about the monetary situation.[61]

The senator from Montana next began to urge large silver purchases on the world market. This tactic had several advantages. It capitalized upon the president's decision to buy domestically produced silver and the belief that increasing the world market price of silver would raise agricultural prices. The latter had declined somewhat in November and December.[62]

Wheeler expected substantial congressional support for purchases on the world market. To be sure, monetary economists refuted the arguments favoring the plan, and during January they could show that gold purchases had failed to lift commodity prices. Their rebuttal lacked force, however, when compared with the political power of the historic convictions they sought to contravene. Moreover, the congressional coalition of silverites and inflationists could expect support from Father Coughlin's thunderous radio voice and the urgings of the Committee for the Nation.[63]

During January, 1934, the president sought to block the emerging drive for mandatory silver legislation by making concessions to the silverites and the inflationists.[64] He talked with Wheeler and King in early January, displaying a "friendly interest" in their arguments for prompt action. King reported that despite the press of official business, Roosevelt had continued the conversation until they had thoroughly covered the silver situation.[65] The senators were flattered by the president's attention, as he had intended, but they were not dissuaded from pressing for prompt action.

Determined to amend the Gold Reserve bill, Wheeler and King

withheld their efforts until after House approval of the president's bill, to secure popular support for a strong stand in the Senate.[66] Their amendment initially required "the purchase of silver up to a billion ounces at a minimum rate of fifty million ounces per month, or until 371 grains of silver [were] equal to 23.22 grains of gold in purchasing power."[67] This draft combined a silver purchase bill proposed by Representative William L. Fiesinger of Ohio, and Senator Wheeler's proposal of "free coinage" as a means to increase the value of silver and lower that of gold. However, the limitation on purchases to one billion ounces would have prevented its restoration to the desired value, and even this proposed maximum was soon lowered to 750 million ounces.[68] The Wheeler-Fiesinger amendment had the support of Senators Borah, Elmer Thomas, and many others. Wheeler was ready for a fight: "It is now or never for silver. If we lose, silver is dead as money for 100 years. We carry the battle flag for people in every nation of the earth. . . . We face our Waterloo on this bill."[69]

On January 22, Wheeler and King discussed their intentions with the president, who said he opposed their amendment since the Thomas amendment had already assigned him the power

> to provide for the unlimited coinage of silver, which, as a practical matter, means that we can take silver in any quantities, from any place in the world, at any price up to $1.29 per ounce. . . . In consequence, no useful end would be served by introducing the complications of the whole subject of silver into Congressional consideration of the Gold Reserve Bill.

Roosevelt offered one minor concession, but the senators felt that it "added nothing to the bill from their standpoint." With this in mind, the president also said that "it will be most fortunate if the Gold Reserve Bill passes without any amendment of any kind relating to silver."[70] Three days later he dictated a "Private and Confidential" note to the Senate Majority Leader, Joseph T. Robinson, instructing him to oppose the Wheeler-Fiesinger proposal because it was "wholly contrary" to his message on the measure. "This is not the time to order the purchase of silver,"

111

he said; "let us wait a little while to see how the Pittman agreement works out."[71] The battle lines were drawn.

On January 27, Senator Wheeler led a spirited debate on his silver purchase amendment. He told the Senate that his primary aim was to find a world market for surplus American products through raising the purchasing power of the silver-using peoples of the Orient. Wheeler also presented the reverse side of this proposition. He claimed that raising the price of silver would also erect a tariff wall against the cheap Japanese and Chinese products coming into the United States. The senator argued that this factor was pertinent because proponents of the Gold Reserve bill frankly asserted that devaluation of the American dollar in terms of gold would restore the barrier to importation of low-cost manufactures from Europe. The senator from Montana said that he was fighting for a principle, not merely for the western silver interests. This was his "firm conviction" as to the effect of higher prices for the white metal on all commodity prices. He compared this objective with the domestic silver program, saying that the latter amounted to a subsidy to the mining interests. "I have never fought for a subsidy."[72]

Several incidents foretold the silver purchase amendment's fate. The majority leader announced that he had a letter opposing the measure from the president. This placed severe pressure on the middle western Democrats, such as J. Hamilton Lewis of Illinois, a former Populist who had voted for remonetization in January, 1933, but who had retreated to the "not voting" column on the same question in April. In the discussion Lewis asked a simple question about the presumed effects of the silver purchase program, which gave Wheeler the opportunity to praise his colleague's considerable knowledge about the matter. "I have sat at his feet to study the silver question," Wheeler said. But the Democrat from Illinois opposed the amendment in the subsequent ballot.[73]

The vote was a surprisingly close forty-three to forty-five. Furthermore, it was reported that had the vote been a tie, had, for instance, Senator Lewis voted "aye" instead of "nay," the vice-president was ready to vote for the Wheeler-Fiesinger amendment.[74] The latter, John Nance Garner, a former congressman from Texas, was at odds with the president, and this gave the report more than the usual credence. However, such speculation tended to falsify the actual situation. The voting was very close only because six Republicans who later voted against the Gold Reserve bill had chosen to support the silver amendment in an effort to embarrass the majority party.[75] On the other hand, a favorable result would have been achieved without these Republican votes had the president not opposed the measure. Borah reported that "at least three men were pulled away from us by pressure from the administration."[76] Also, he later told a silver producer from Idaho, James P. McCarthy:

We would have carried the silver proposition unquestionably by a good majority had not the administration made every effort to defeat it. But I am of the opinion it will come up again before the session closes. I do not believe the administration can defeat it again.[77]

The Silver Bloc's prospects for future advances were measurably improved immediately after the close silver purchase vote. Senator Pittman proposed and obtained quick acceptance of an amendment to the Gold Reserve bill which augmented the president's permissive authority with respect to silver coinage. He told his colleagues that the amendment's important features included permission to mint the metal obtained as seigniorage and the "issuance [of] silver certificates against any other silver bullion or silver dollars . . . which may come into the Treasury hereafter."[78] Pittman emphasized the significance of the latter item.

I reserve the right to offer a separate bill later on to carry out certain features of what I have in view, but I do not desire to embarrass the Banking and Currency committee, or the Senate, by suggesting anything which might be thought would cause delay of the Gold Reserve Bill, either on the floor of the Senate or in conference.[79]

A few minutes later, the entire measure received approval.[80]

Pittman's actions later that day indicated that he was troubled by either conflicting loyalties or political pressures. He argued and voted for the Wheeler amendment in the Senate. Shortly after its defeat and the acceptance of his own amendment, however, he informed the president by telephone that the new measure was "innocuous," and that he had "cast one vote [for Wheeler's proposal] today with the understanding that if the motion had carried he would move for reconsideration, then vote against it."[81] If the Nevada senator was not caught between obligations, he certainly sought to give Roosevelt that impression. The element of strain in their relationship was increasingly evident during the course of 1934.[82] That fall, Democrats Pittman, Wheeler, King, Ashurst, and Erickson were to stand for reelection.

The gold bill episode seemed to clear the air about the silver movement. The fourteen silver senators had voted as a bloc for the first time. Most important was the agreement by Borah, Pittman, Wheeler, and Elmer Thomas on the strategic advantage of silver purchase legislation. Previously, Borah had been opposed, Wheeler disdainful, and Thomas disinterested, while Pittman alone pushed for a federal subsidy. Then, in January, 1934, Pittman seemingly hesitated to vote for Wheeler's silver purchase scheme, which Borah and Thomas supported. But they were moving on the same path.

The differences between the western senators further diminished following the presidential proclamation of January 31, 1934, which nationalized gold and devalued the dollar.[83] Thereafter, these legislators concentrated on incorporating silver into the restructured monetary policy. While members of the Silver Bloc and the Farm Bloc continued to argue over the need for inflation, they worked together for expansion of the money supply through silver purchase legislation.

1. Shover, *Cornbelt Rebellion*, p. 147.
2. Schlesinger, *Coming of the New Deal*, p. 236.
3. Thomas, "Forty Years a Legislator," *passim*.
4. Elmer Thomas, *Financial Engineering* (Washington: published privately, 1953), *passim*.

5. Wesley McCune, *Farm Bloc* (Garden City, New York: Doubleday, Doran & Co., 1943), p. 40.

6. Thomas to author, May 20, 1963.

7. Fred I. Kent, "The Mystery of the Gold Standard," *Literary Digest,* CXVI (July, 1933), 5, 32–33.

8. Thomas to Kent, August 4, 1933, Thomas Papers, box 460, Money—currency expansion file.

9. *New York Times,* September 20, 21, 1933.

10. *Boston Evening News,* September 19, 1933. For a discussion of the relationship of this agitation to the general agricultural situation see Van L. Perkins, "The AAA and the Politics of Agriculture: Agricultural Policy Formulation in the Fall of 1933," *Agricultural History,* XXXIX (October, 1965), 220–29.

11. *New York Times,* October 25, 1933.

12. Thomas to Black, August 20, 1933, E. Thomas Papers, box 456, Money—conference file.

13. Elmer Thomas, "Money and Its Management," *Annals of the American Academy of Political and Social Science,* CLXXI (January, 1934), 137; Mitchell to Thomas, February 3, 1933, E. Thomas Papers, box 459, Money—currency expansion file.

14. *New York Times,* December 21, 1933.

15. *Ibid.,* December 22, 1933.

16. Le Blanc to Thomas, July 31, 1933, E. Thomas Papers, box 458, Money—currency expansion file. Thomas concedes that Le Blanc "was very helpful with suggestions as to the end to be attained—more money, cheaper money and higher prices." Thomas to author, May 20, 1963.

17. Charles J. Tull, *Father Coughlin and the New Deal* (New York: Syracuse University Press, 1965), p. 21.

18. Coughlin to Roosevelt, November 17, 1933, Roosevelt Papers, POF 306, box 1. On September 24, 1933, the priest said that "last week alone I received sixty-six bags of mail."

19. Coughlin to Early, November 14, 1933, Roosevelt Papers, POF 306, box 1. At the president's request the Royal Oak, Michigan, post office confirmed the priest's claims. Tull, p. 41.

20. Charles E. Coughlin, *The New Deal in Money* (Royal Oak, Michigan: Radio League of the Little Flower, 1933), pp. 12, 40, 45.

21. *Ibid.,* p. 49. Coughlin probably did not know that the monetary value of silver was $1.29 per ounce.

22. Coughlin to Thomas, November 15, 1933, E. Thomas Papers, box 399, Special correspondence file.

23. *New York Times,* September 15, 1933.

24. *Rocky Mountain News* (Denver), November 18, 1933; *New York Times,* November 27, 1933; Pittman to Franklin D. Roosevelt, November 15, 1933, Pittman Papers, box 142, Government Departments folder. He included a copy of his explication with this letter.

25. *Rocky Mountain News* (Denver), November 18, 1933; *New York Times,* November 27, 1933.

26. Acheson, pp. 174–75. Roosevelt requested Acheson's resignation as under secretary of the Treasury during this embroglio.

27. Bernard M. Baruch, "The Dangers of Inflation," *Saturday Evening Post,* CCVI (November 25, 1933), 5, 87.

28. *New York Times,* November 22, 1933.

29. For a thorough examination of this controversy, see: Johnson, *The Treasury and Monetary Policy*, pp. 18–28.

30. *New York Times*, November 25, 1933.

31. Schlesinger, *Coming of the New Deal*, pp. 244–45.

32. *New York Times*, November 25, 1933.

33. *Ibid.*, November 23, 1933.

34. *Ibid.*, November 28, 1933; Tull, *Father Coughlin*, pp. 56–57.

35. Thomas to Coughlin, December 5, 1933, E. Thomas Papers, box 399, Special correspondence file.

36. Byrnes to Roosevelt, December 2, 1933, Roosevelt Papers, POF 229, box 4.

37. Jeanette P. Nichols, "Silver Inflation and the Senate in 1933," *Social Studies*, XXV (January, 1934), 17.

38. *New York Times*, October 25, 1933. It is not suggested that the sequestration proposal originated with Thomas. Rather, his advocacy advanced the timing of its initiation to some extent. Undoubtedly, the fact that the gold buying experiment had not improved price levels as had been hoped also did much to determine the timing of the gold sequestration.

39. Coughlin to Thomas, November 15, 1933, E. Thomas Papers, box 399, Special correspondence file.

40. Roosevelt to House, November 21, 1933, in Roosevelt (ed.), *F.D.R., His Personal Letters*, III, 373.

41. Johnson, *Treasury and Monetary Policy*, pp. 10–28.

42. *New York Times*, December 22, 1933. The sequestration proposal was ignored when Thomas first mentioned it at a conference in Washington, October 25, 1933.

43. Thomas to Coughlin, January 6, 1934, E. Thomas Papers, box 459, Money—currency expansion file.

44. Tull, p. 51.   45. *New York Times*, January 7, 8, 1934.

46. *Ibid.*, December 23, 1933. On December 22 the members of the Federal Reserve Board discussed this matter for eight hours.

47. *Ibid.*, December 22, 1933. Krock attributes the sequestration idea to Thomas and James Harvey Rogers, a professor of economics at Yale and a presidential advisor at that time.

48. Johnson, *Treasury and Monetary Policy*, p. 30. Eugene R. Black, governor of the Federal Reserve Board, made a statement on the board's position with regard to the Gold Reserve bill to the Senate Committee on Banking and Currency. Black outlined but understated his objections to the bill. *New York Times*, January 19, 1934.

49. U.S., *Congressional Record*, 73d Cong., 2d Sess., 1934, LXXVIII, Part 1 (January 15, 1934), 614–15.

50. The British Treasury operated an Equalization Account to assist devaluation of the pound sterling in 1932 and 1933. Johnson, *Treasury and Monetary Policy*, pp. 85–88.

51. U.S., *Statutes at Large*, XLVIII, Part 1, Public Law No. 87, 337.

52. *New York Times*, January 8, 1934.

53. John M. Blum, *From the Morgenthau Diaries*, I, *Years of Crisis, 1929–1938* (Boston: Houghton Mifflin Company, 1959), 124–25.

54. Johnson, *Treasury and Monetary Policy*, pp. 37–38.

55. *Commercial and Financial Chronicle*, January 20, 1934.

56. *New York Times*, January 16, 1934.

57. U.S., *Congressional Record*, 73d Cong., 2d Sess., 1934, LXXVIII, Part 1 (January 15, 1934), 615.

58. *Ibid.*
59. The statutory price for monetary silver was $1.29 per ounce. After devaluation, the price at the sixteen to one ratio would be $2.19 per ounce.
60. *New York Herald-Tribune,* December 30, 1933. This article is by Ernest K. Lindley. The *Philadelphia Herald-Inquirer's* list of names and positions is more accurate than that in the *Herald-Tribune.* At a meeting in King's office on December 29, eighteen were present and approved, nine were absent but favored by proxy, and seventeen others were absent but were reported to be sympathetic. *Philadelphia Herald-Inquirer,* December 30, 1933.
61. Burton K. Wheeler to author, September 22, 1961.
62. Schlesinger, *Coming of the New Deal,* p. 246.
63. Thomas to Coughlin, January 9, 1934, E. Thomas Papers, box 399, Special correspondence file. Thomas invited the priest to Washington on January 15 for "a conference relative to the money situation. I do not think this conference should be too liberally attended."
64. Everest, *Morgenthau, The New Deal, and Silver,* p. 39.
65. *Salt Lake Tribune,* January 5, 1934. King gave a special interview to the reporter, Harry J. Brown.
66. *New York Times,* January 22, 1934.
67. Memorandum, Franklin D. Roosevelt, January 22, 1934, Roosevelt Papers, POF 229, box 5; U.S., *Congressional Record,* 73d Cong., 2d Sess., 1934, LXXVIII, Part 2 (January 26, 1934), 1414–15.
68. U.S., *Congressional Record,* 73d Cong., 2d Sess., 1934, LXXVIII, Part 2 (January 27, 1934), 1464.
69. *Denver Post,* January 22, 1934.
70. Memorandum, Franklin D. Roosevelt, January 22, 1934, Roosevelt Papers, POF 229, box 5.
71. Roosevelt to Robinson, January 25, 1934, Roosevelt Papers, POF 229, box 5.
72. U.S., *Congressional Record,* 73d Cong., 2d Sess., 1934, LXXVIII, Part 2 (January 27, 1934), 1448–50. Economists generally note that any rise in American trade barriers lowered our trading partners' purchasing power, a fact which Wheeler chose to overlook. Also, conditions in China at that time negated Wheeler's contentions. That nation's balance of payments' deficit was a serious problem by the end of 1933. Wei-Ying Lin, *The New Monetary System of China: A Personal Interpretation* (Chicago: The University of Chicago Press, 1936), p. 25.
73. U.S., *Congressional Record,* 73d Cong., 2d Sess., 1934, LXXVIII, Part 2 (January 27, 1934), 1462, 1464–65.
74. *Denver Post,* January 28, 1934. This matter was discussed by Charles O. Gridley, a special correspondent. It was not otherwise verified.
75. The six Republicans were: James J. Davis, Pennsylvania; John L. Dickinson, Iowa; Charles L. McNary, Oregon; Arthur R. Robinson, Indiana; Frederick Steiwer, Oregon; and John G. Townsend, Delaware.
76. Borah to John H. Worms, January 29, 1934, Borah Papers, box 374, Silver folder.
77. Borah to McCarthy, January 31, 1934, Borah Papers, box 374, Silver folder.
78. U.S., *Congressional Record,* 73d Cong., 2d Sess., 1934, LXXVIII, Part 2 (January 27, 1934), 1475.
79. *Ibid.,* 1474.   80. *Ibid.,* 1484.
81. Marvin McIntyre to Roosevelt, January 27, 1934, Roosevelt Papers, POF 229, box 5.

82. Israel has emphasized the dicordant factors in their relationship. See his chapter 5, titled "Becoming Somewhat Opposed to Roosevelt," pp. 96–139.

83. U.S., *Statutes at Large*, XLVIII, Part 2, Proclamation No. 2072, 1730–31.

7 The Silver Purchase Act

In the spring of 1934, demands for silver purchase legislation became intense. The recent close Senate vote on the Wheeler-Fiesinger amendment to the Gold Reserve Act encouraged the silverites and inflationists. Being unable to restore bimetallism, they pressed the Congress for legislation requiring substantial purchases of the white metal for the monetary system. Lobbyists on Capitol Hill representing agriculture, mining, and other economic interests, including speculators in the metal, willingly supported its advocates. The Silver Bloc sought and won help from the president. The result was the Silver Purchase Act of 1934.

The House of Representatives forged the first link in the chain of circumstances leading to new silver legislation. On February 2, 1934, Congressman Martin L. Dies of Texas, a state producing cotton, wheat, and silver, introduced a bill authorizing the establishment of an Agricultural Surplus and Exchange Board to negotiate the disposal of surpluses, to accept silver in exchange therefor at a value not to exceed 25 percent more than the world market price, and to deposit such metal with the secretary of the Treasury. The latter was authorized to coin this bullion and use it as a basis for the issue of silver certificates.[1] As in the case of the Thomas amendment, Dies' measure drew together the advocates of silver, monetary inflation, and higher prices for agricultural commodities. Following hearings, the Committee on Coinage, Weights and Measures reported the bill favorably on March 16, 1934, at the request of the speaker, Henry L. Rainey of Illinois.[2] The chairman of that committee, Andrew L. Somers

119

of New York, readily agreed when Rainey decided to schedule the bill for a vote under a suspension of the rules.[3]

The speaker's prompt action was a deliberate affront to the Roosevelt administration in retaliation for its earlier legislative maneuvers on the Gold Reserve bill. With the president's tacit approval, the chairman of the Banking and Currency Committee introduced a duplicate bill as a substitute to a measure pending in the House. His action avoided the probable addition of a silver amendment by the Committee on Coinage, Weights and Measures, to which Rainey had assigned the original draft despite his knowledge of the president's disapproval.[4] The incident doubly offended the speaker because it slighted his official prerogatives as leader of the House and ignored his personal preferences on the silver issue.[5]

The more immediate cause of Rainey's ire was a remark attributed to Secretary Morgenthau. At a press conference held shortly after he met with Representative Somers and several members of the Committee on Coinage, the secretary mentioned that, in reference to an investigation by his department into silver speculation, "we have found some [silver advocates] that were not disinterested."[6] He failed to anticipate that at least a large minority of the congressmen considered themselves to be proponents of the metal at that time; nor did he realize that many silverites believed themselves to be the victims of Wall Street speculators. Perhaps it was the president's awareness of bruised congressional sensibilities that stayed his intervention before the Dies bill vote.[7] On March 19, the measure was approved 257 to 112.[8]

While the speaker's distaste for Morgenthau's verbal indiscretion undoubtedly was genuine, the readiness of the House to adopt the Dies bill indicated that more substantial forces also were involved. Earlier, Congressman James G. Scrugham of Nevada had organized approximately a hundred of his colleagues into a group supporting silver legislation.[9] These individuals had little or no difficulty in obtaining additional votes—as the 257 "ayes" indicated—when mining and agricultural interests worked in concert. Certainly, this strength extended far beyond the thinly populated states that produced the white metal. That fact was further emphasized when on March 20, Elmer Thomas of Oklahoma asked the Senate to refer the Dies bill to the Committee on Agriculture and Forestry.[10]

The proposal by Congressman Dies to exchange agricultural surpluses for silver failed to satisfy most members of the Senate Silver Bloc. Newspaper reports said that a majority of them believed the president would veto the bill should it be approved by the Senate, while some of them objected because the measure treated silver as a commodity and not as a primary money. On March 24, twenty-four western and southern legislators met to formally organize a caucus and to select a steering committee. The group named King, who had called the meeting, chairman, and he selected six colleagues for his committee: Borah, Wheeler, Adams, McCarran, Henrik I. Shipstead of Minnesota (the Farmer-Labor party's lone senator), plus a Republican reelected in 1932, Frederick Stiewer of Oregon. The group tried to write a substitute for the Dies bill, but their differences frustrated all efforts to devise an acceptable revision.[11]

Whereas the senatorial caucus was unable to devise an alternative to the Dies bill, the Committee on Agriculture succeeded. Several senators proposed additional features relevant to the metal. On April 8, Elmer Thomas told of his proposed amendment authorizing the nationalization of all domestic stocks and the issue of a large quantity of silver certificates backed by that acquisition. He sought not only additional support for the measure but he also wanted to force a "showdown" with the president on expansion of the money supply.[12] The following day, moreover, a group of senators led by Pittman revised Dies' original measure authorizing the barter of agricultural surpluses for silver, a proposal directing the purchase of fifty million ounces of silver a month until silver's world market price reached $1.29 per ounce.[13] The Committee on Agriculture adopted this version the following day, and then appended to it the nationalization requirement offered by Thomas.[14] Its provisions ensured strong congressional support.

Senator Thomas told reporters the objectives of the revised bill. Its purposes were (1) to dispose of agricultural surpluses;

121

(2) to increase the price of silver and open markets in silver-using countries; (3) to put new money in the hands of producers; and (4) to retain agricultural markets for American producers. As to his future strategy, Thomas said that, if necessary, he would offer this compendium as an amendment.[15]

The Silver Bloc refused to support the revised Dies bill. King immediately rejected the measure as being too inflationary, and Borah requested further study because inflation would necessarily imply a de-emphasis on silver. Furthermore, he doubted that Republicans would support it, as they had the Wheeler amendment, merely in an effort to oppose the president.[16]

On April 12, 1934, King announced a meeting of the steering committee to devise amendments to the Dies bill. Also, he was invited to lunch with the president, at which time they would talk about silver. The luncheon invitation indicated the president's hope to avoid an impasse with the Silver Bloc, and King's announcement implied a willingness to compromise even while Elmer Thomas asserted: "We are going to fight this thing to the finish and do it now."[17]

Silverites were divided, but Elmer Thomas knew that many of his colleagues either favored or were sure to vote for the Dies bill. It seemed likely to gain a majority, but certain to be blocked by the president. Would he make an attempt in that election year to forestall a veto?

Support for the Dies bill increased pressures on the president to take the initiative. At first he seemed to oppose any new legislation. Those who doubted his opposition were hard pressed to explain the Treasury's investigation of speculation in the white metal. At the same time, Roosevelt, a facile political leader, enjoyed an undisputable popularity. Perhaps he wished to appear beset by irresistible demands, hoping to placate some critics of his monetary actions. The president failed to record his motives and the effects of the pressures upon him. His alternatives were somewhat limited by the silverites' determination, but the Silver Bloc's several accomplishments suggested that Roosevelt was more than sympathetic.

On April 14, 1934, the president discussed pending legislation with sixteen leaders in the Senate including Pittman, Wheeler, Clarence C. Dill of Washington, and "Cotton Ed" Smith. Of more than a dozen topics covered in their survey, silver was the most troublesome. Pittman contested the president's views on the subject. Their discussion was detailed but inconclusive. Finally, Roosevelt asked Pittman for more time in order to reach an international agreement on silver.[18]

There were two contradictory sources of information on Pittman's disagreement with the president; each was written from a different perspective. A presidential assistant prepared the more detailed account, which emphasized the president's remarks, giving the impression that Roosevelt was firmly opposed to silver legislation at that time.[19] The other, a comparatively brief account on their discussion, was written by a reporter for the *Salt Lake Tribune* who interviewed Pittman shortly after the conference. Pittman reportedly said that the president admitted he was "up a tree" on the silver question and therefore desired a bill that he could approve. Roosevelt acknowledged the existence of strong congressional support for silver legislation according to the senator, and said he was willing to "talk things over" with representatives of the Silver Bloc. The reporter also noted that the legislative leaders expected new silver legislation during that session of the Congress.[20]

The president sought accommodation with the Bloc. On April 17, 1934, King briefly discussed the prospects with him, and they scheduled a meeting with the steering committee for the following week.[21] This procedure irritated Wheeler and Elmer Thomas because they believed that consultation on this issue would be a mistake, and unlikely to produce mandatory legislation. Neither had forgotten Roosevelt's limited use of the Thomas amendment powers a year earlier. Like Borah, they preferred to present the president with a bill after it passed the Senate; then he could do as he pleased. Upon learning about this, Roosevelt telephoned Borah and asked him to attend the conference with King's committee.[22]

The conference at the White House presented all the elements of a confrontation between the power and perquisites of the executive and legislative branches. It brought face to face men with opposed and deeply held convictions involved in a struggle over monetary beliefs, economic principles, political responsibilities, and regional loyalties. Present at this gathering on April 21, in addition to the president, were his monetary advisors including Henry Morgenthau, Herman Oliphant, Eugene Black of the Federal Reserve Board, and Bryan Patton Harrison of Mississippi, chairman of the Senate's Committee on Finance. The silver senators included five members of the Bloc's steering committee, Borah, King, McCarran, Adams, and Shipstead, plus Pittman and Elmer Thomas.[23] Wheeler was conspicuous by his absence.

Although the conferees talked longer than an hour, the only decision made was to arrange another meeting. The president, King, Pittman, and Thomas led the discussion. Roosevelt reiterated his opposition to mandatory legislation, especially the Dies bill. The senators, on the other hand, rejected any merely permissive measure.[24] Immediately after this conference, McCarran said they received little consolation from the meeting, while King was hopeful, and Thomas was ready for battle. Thomas suggested that a bill might be constructed with both mandatory and permissive powers.[25]

The conference seemed to produce a deadlock, but the senators recognized the president's readiness to bargain; this could only work to their advantage. However, a few of their number voiced the opinion that Roosevelt had outmaneuvered them, and one asserted that they were determined not to permit the same occurrence at any subsequent conference.[26]

The senators used every available opportunity to display their grievance over Roosevelt's opposition to mandatory legislation. On April 23, 1934, the Committee on Agriculture held an open meeting attended by the Silver Bloc and other partisans of the metal. Thomas, Borah, and Pittman dominated the group. Father Coughlin also attended and spoke briefly but provocatively, demanding immediate action. Thomas and Borah agreed with the priest's assertion that the Congress should act independently on pending silver legislation. Pittman, on the other hand, asked for moderation and cooperation with the president.[27]

The senator from Nevada privately urged Roosevelt to seek a compromise. In a letter written two days after the meeting called by the Committee on Agriculture, he pointed out the probable consequences of noncooperation.

No doubt . . . the Dies Bill will pass the Senate either with the present silver amendments or with some others. The result will be unfortunate in any case. If you should sign the bill you would sign an imperfect act, which might be internationally disturbing. If you vetoed the act, and it could not be carried over your veto in the Senate, it would undoubtedly embarrass members of the House and Senate in their support of your program in the coming campaign.[28]

During the last third of April the Silver Bloc seemed to gain added public support. On the evening of April 23, upwards of two hundred members of the House and Senate attended a dinner given by the Committee for the Nation to dramatize the strong congressional support for the Dies bill. [29] A congressional liaison reported to Morgenthau that "Cotton Ed" Smith was one of the sponsors of this gathering.[30] Another favorable sign for silverites resulted from the publication of a long list of individuals, corporations, and banking institutions speculating in silver.[31] Its release had coincided with the Committee for the Nation's congressional dinner. Despite extensive newspaper comment in the East, these revelations failed to arouse more than passing public interest. Holdings of silver by individuals were miniscule compared with those of corporations and banks. On balance, this, too, was a favorable event for the silverites.[32]

Other events late in April increased the pressures for silver legislation. The president discussed this problem with his cabinet, asking his department heads what they thought about the issue. A majority favored compromise. Their general opinion, according to Morgenthau, was that the veto of "another important measure would be most embarrassing at election time."[33] The following day, Henry A. Wallace, the secretary of Agriculture, wrote to the president about the Dies bill and its probable effect on farm prices. Wallace ended his letter by noting that he had "discovered in conversation with two Democratic senators last night that the sentiment in the Senate is unusually strong for the Dies bill. Apparently even some of the conservative Democratic senators will be inclined to vote for it."[34]

With expectations running in the Silver Bloc's favor, Key Pittman swapped pointed little stories with the president. Each told the other an amusing fable which pointed up his own position with regard to silver as money. The senator led off the exchange when he wrote:

There was a breed of monkeys 'way back in the Malay jungle. There were only a few of them, and they had lived in a very small space during all of their generations. There was only one thing that they would eat, and that was a little pomegranate— a little golden pomegranate. And then along came a big fire that destroyed the entire area where these golden pomegranates grew. The little monkeys were starving, and other monkeys did their best to get them to eat other pomegranates. There was a beautiful silver pomegranate, just as delicious as the gold pomegranate, which all the other monkeys in the Malay Peninsula had grown fat on; but the little golden monkeys would not eat anything but the little golden pomegranates. And today they are all dead.

The president replied in the same manner a few days later:

The true story runs this way. It was perfectly true that the little monkeys got on very well with their little golden pomegranates. After the big fire destroyed the golden pomegranates the little monkeys discovered vast quantities of silver pomegranates. They liked them so well that they ate dozens and dozens of them and that is why all the little monkeys are dead today![35]

Roosevelt, seeking a compromise agreement, turned to a proposal submitted by Pittman. It suggested a way to justify substantial increases in the monetary stocks of silver without resort to bimetallism. He proposed that the balance of the metallic reserves be returned to the proportions obtaining in 1900, or approximately 30 percent silver and 70 percent gold.[36] Late in April,

Roosevelt briefly referred to this idea when talking with Congressman James G. Scrugham of Nevada and five of his colleagues. The president said that the current 12 percent silver and 88 percent gold in the metallic reserves could safely be altered to a thirty-seventy ratio.[37] Soon afterward, Pittman explained this matter to reporters.

> In 1900, 30 per cent of our currency was silver, while 70 per cent was gold. Today, basing our currency on gold at $35 per ounce, only 12 per cent of our currency is silver. I urged that the restoration of the balance of our currency was purely a national act and was no concern of any foreign country. While the President would not commit himself on this subject, he . . . indicated no opposition to the restoration of such a balance in our currency.[38]

The senator was referring to his remarks at the conference held two weeks earlier, although he publicized this matter only after Roosevelt had talked with Scrugham. It was probable that meanwhile Herman Oliphant had been investigating the proposal.[39]

Key Pittman added a second important proposition to his thirty-seventy formula. On April 25, he urged the president to search actively for a legislative compromise, particularly with reference to mandatory versus discretionary legislation. He suggested: "I believe that we can work out amendments to the silver provision of the Dies Bill, which while in expression are mandatory, will, in fact, be so flexible and so limited as to avoid entirely the dangers of mandatory legislation which you fear."[40]

By the end of April the elements for compromise between the president and the Silver Bloc were known to each party. In the following weeks the issues were arranged to make them acceptable to a majority of those immediately concerned. Missing was a situation that required prompt presidential action.

At this juncture, Elmer Thomas challenged the president. On May 2, 1934, as the Senate prepared to take final action on the Industrial Loans bill proposed by Carter Glass, Thomas halted the Senate's proceedings by offering an amendment which established a comprehensive policy on silver. Admittedly, Thomas sought to force the president either to reject his amendment or to negotiate an acceptable alternative. Thomas' measure combined Congressman Dies' proposal to exchange surplus commodities for silver with nationalization of that metal, a discretionary authorization to purchase silver, and a mandatory thirty-seventy balance in the reserves of silver and gold.[41] Because of its appeal in the Senate, this measure required either the president's intervention or a later exercise of his veto power.

Roosevelt responded by arranging another meeting with the Bloc, intimating that Thomas' compendium would be the basis of their discussion. Pittman, Borah, Wheeler, King, Shipstead, Adams, Dill, Smith, and Thomas met the day before that meeting and agreed to support Thomas' most recent amendment, minus the proposal to export surplus commodities in exchange for silver.[42] On May 5, they presented the measure to the president. He made no promises, but he was more sympathetic than at their previous meeting and Thomas agreed to withdraw his amendment to the Glass bill.[43]

In the following weeks, the administration and the Bloc wrote an acceptable bill. On May 8, Roosevelt and the senators agreed on the general terms. These included increasing the quantity of monetary silver to one-fourth that of gold in terms of value, nationalization of all stocks of the metal, and the assurance of purchases which would be discretionary as to time and amount. The following day, however, Morgenthau met with them and refused to consider the statement of policy requiring purchases, which the president had accepted in principle. Borah bolted from this meeting and told waiting reporters that he thought the entire matter should be dropped until after the election campaign that fall. Morgenthau quickly consulted with Roosevelt, then reversed himself and directed Oliphant to draft a measure based upon the senators' understanding of the agreement, including a statement that acquisitions of the metal would be mandatory.[44]

The president was conciliatory at his final meeting with the Silver Bloc the following week, dropping his previous insistence that he remain entirely free from commitment. Both Roosevelt and Morgenthau agreed that the authority to purchase silver would be executed "enthusiastically" if, in return, the amount and timing of purchases remained flexible. Also, the senators agreed to a 50 percent tax on speculative profits in trading on silver, although they objected to the stipulation. Finally, Roosevelt said he would tell Democrats in the Congress to vote for the measure.[45]

Following the Silver Bloc's final conference with Roosevelt, its members returned to their characteristic disagreement over objectives. They had avoided public conflicts throughout April and early May. Immediately, Borah, Wheeler, McCarran, and Elmer Thomas expressed strong dissatisfaction with the administration's proposal, and promised to improve it with amendments.[46] Probably each realized such efforts would be futile. Borah admitted privately to Congressman Fiesinger that the measure could not be amended in either the House or the Senate: "It is the only legislation that is possible at this session."[47]

Elmer Thomas led the dissidents' attack on the silver purchase bill. On June 2, he sent a lengthy, detailed letter explaining his objections to the majority leader. Thomas complained that the bill as drafted by the Treasury Department, more precisely by Oliphant in consultation with Pittman, failed: to change the status of silver to that of a basic money; to guarantee the expansion of the money supply in circulation through the issuance of silver certificates; and to eliminate the tax on the profits from silver transactions.[48] The unhappy senator found no reassurance in Robinson's reply.

I shall, of course, be glad to devote my best efforts to reconciling the differences, but it is a little discouraging to undertake such a task considering that others better informed respecting the whole subject involved have failed after the most painstaking and persistent efforts.[49]

This dispute led to yet another conference. The participants were Thomas, Borah, Wheeler, Pittman, and Oliphant. Their discussion centered upon the administration's demand for a 50 percent transfer tax. According to Professor Blum, the purpose of that provision was to limit the gains of those who had bought silver speculatively and then lobbied for a subsidy. As Secretary Morgenthau [had] told the press, "we are not going to let fifteen or twenty people clean up twenty-five or fifty million dollars through a monetary program of the Government!"[50]

Among the five senators at this meeting, only Pittman defended the administration's position. Afterward, he conveyed his colleagues' objections to Roosevelt, but the tax remained in the measure.[51]

The silver purchase bill made swift progress through the legislative machinery. Roosevelt sent it to the House on May 22, 1934, requesting that it be adopted forthwith.[52] It was introduced the following day by Congressman Martin L. Dies and passed without amendment on May 31, but not without damage to a number of political egos.[53] In the Senate, Key Pittman received permission to read the measure twice and lay it on the table.[54] This maneuver prevented revisions by the Committee on Banking and Currency.

Pittman guided and guarded the silver purchase bill throughout its ordeal in the Senate. Not only was he the logical choice among the senators for this task, he had asked for the assignment. The day following Roosevelt's final conference with the Bloc, Pittman presented a lengthy résumé of his qualifications for this honor in a letter to Morgenthau. He told of his efforts to shape the measure, but he made no assertions of paternity, noting that King and Borah had authorship claims equal to his own. Characteristically, he based his arguments on expediency and tactical considerations, telling Morgenthau that the task required someone able to present and defend the bill with accuracy and without possible harmful exaggeration about the effects of its implementation. Furthermore, his introduction of the measure would be "acceptable to the East and the gold standard advocates," Pittman claimed, and to his western colleagues as well.

I have a great ambition, as a closing act in the work that I have been doing with regard to silver during the past five years, to offer this amendment. I feel that this would be more agreeable to the Silver Bloc than to have any other member of the Silver Bloc offer it.[55]

Pittman successfully obstructed all senatorial efforts to amend the measure. Its outright opponents were few and ineffectual. Their only hope lay in upsetting the Bloc's agreement with Roosevelt, but they completely failed in this endeavor. Even the strengthening amendments offered by Elmer Thomas, McCarran, and Huey Long were easily defeated. The Senate adopted it by a fifty-five to twenty-five margin on June 11, 1934.[56]

The main provisions of the Silver Purchase Act of 1934 declared[57] that: (1) the proportion of silver to gold in the monetary stocks should be increased until the monetary value in silver equaled one-fourth[58] of such stocks; (2) the secretary of the Treasury should purchase silver, at his own discretion regarding the time and the price, until the monetary stocks were balanced at one-fourth silver to three-fourths gold, or until the market price of silver reached $1.29 per ounce; (3) he must issue silver certificates to equal at least the amount paid for such silver; (4) the president could nationalize domestic silver stocks at a price not to exceed fifty cents per ounce; (5) the secretary of the Treasury must assess a 50 percent tax on all profits above original costs made through transfers of silver.[59] In addition to assuring silver producers a market, the act subjected the production and distribution of silver in the United States to rigid governmental supervision.[60] While the major producers enjoyed the marketing certainties it established, their lesser competitors doubtlessly foresaw needless time and profit losses made unavoidable by regulated dealings with the government.

Senate adoption of the Silver Purchase Act produced strong feelings among persons associated with the silver movement. These reactions varied strikingly with the objectives pursued by each of them. Key Pittman was elated and he immediately sent telegrams to four newspapers in Nevada beginning: "SENATOR PITTMAN SUCCESSFULLY STEERED THE SILVER BILL THROUGH THE SENATE TODAY AFTER A DRAMATIC FIGHT."[61] Borah later revealed in a letter to Irvin Rockwell that he left the Senate with

131

"a touch of gloom" because the act did not deal with the silver question.[62] Wheeler's opinion was not recorded, but a short time later he resumed advocacy of bimetallism.[63] Perhaps he agreed with the reaction of Caroline Evans of the Bimetallic Association, who complained to Borah that the measure was not a step in the right direction because it destroyed the movement for remonetization.[64]

Editorialists expressed relief because the Silver Purchase Act avoided both bimetallism and mandatory terminology. The editors of the *Boston Evening Transcript* said it was unlikely that Roosevelt would order more than "moderate purchases" of the metal, and they expected little increase in silver prices.[65] The editors of the *New York Times* expressed similar views but regretted that an unnecessary "sop" had been thrown to the silverites.[66]

The Silver Purchase Act of 1934 marked the high point in the Silver Bloc's legislative drive. Despite complaints from some advocates of the metal that the act neither went far enough nor answered the silver question, subsequent proposals failed to win the Bloc's support. Its members rejected bimetallism and the substantial monetary inflation sought by Elmer Thomas. However, the senators watched carefully to see that the Roosevelt administration enforced the newly adopted silver program.

Implementation of the Silver Purchase Act would be directed by Secretary Morgenthau, who had promised to execute its mandate "enthusiastically." In the latter months of 1934, the senators began to have doubts; soon, conflict emerged over the Treasury's silver policies.

1. U.S., *Congressional Record*, 73d Cong., 2d Sess., 1934, LXXVIII, Part 2 (February 2, 1934), 1895.
2. U.S., Congress, House of Representatives, Committee on Coinage, Weights and Measures, *Report, Exchange of Agricultural Surplus for Silver*, Report No. 992, 73d Cong., 2d Sess., 1934, p. 1.
3. *New York Times*, March 17, 1934.
4. *Ibid.*, January 15, 16, 17, 18, 1934.
5. "I am a sixteen to oner, an old fashioned Bryan silver man," Rainey told newsmen on April 17, 1933. *Ibid.*, April 18, 1933. His views were well known to the administration and the public. *Ibid.*, December 31, 1933.
6. *Ibid.*, March 16, 1934. Others have reported on this investigation in

detail. Everest has noted that "the Senators resented the implication that their own body was influenced by speculation, and they developed a strong antipathy to the investigation." Everest also said that due to "the reports of vast hoards of silver in New York bank vaults, Morgenthau early in February ordered Treasury agents to obtain from the Commodity Exchange and the banks connected with it the names of large holders of the metal." Everest, *Morgenthau, The New Deal, and Silver,* pp. 40–41. The complete list of speculators in the Morgenthau Diaries is closed to researchers, but some of its contents were published in the *New York Times,* April 25, 26, 27, 1934. The lists indicate that a number of New York banks held on their own account vast stores of silver bullion. Though few in numbers, these banks were the major dollar beneficiaries of speculatively held silver stocks nationalized by the federal government on August 9, 1934, under the terms of the Silver Purchase Act of 1934. It is not here asserted that the banks were "silver advocates" as was Father Charles E. Coughlin. The priest's Radio League of the Little Flower had invested $20,000 in spot silver (approximately 500,000 ounces). Coughlin said that no silver was held in his name or for his personal benefit. *New York Times,* April 29, 1934. It is less surprising perhaps that William Jennings Bryan, Jr., held 100,000 ounces of silver in futures contracts. U.S., Congress, Senate, *Hoarders of Silver,* Senate Document No. 173, 73d Cong., 2d Sess., 1934, pp. 6, 33.

7. On March 17, two days before the vote, Rainey spoke by telephone with the president about pending legislation. Neither mentioned this upcoming event. *Salt Lake Tribune,* March 18, 1934.

8. U.S., *Congressional Record,* 73d Cong., 2d Sess., 1934, LXXVIII, Part 5 (March 19, 1934), 4863.

9. James G. Scrugham to Edward C. Walker, March 7, 1934, Henry H. Blood Papers (Utah State Governors File, Utah State Historical Society, Salt Lake City, Utah), box 22, Western Governors Conference. Hereafter cited as Blood Papers.

10. U.S., *Congressional Record,* 73d Cong., 2d Sess., 1934, LXXVIII, Part 5 (March 20, 1934), 4873.

11. *Salt Lake Tribune,* March 23, 24, 25, 26, 27, 1934. This series of articles was written by a *Tribune* special correspondent with whom Senator King frequently discussed the progress of legislation. Pittman did not join this group in a formal way.

12. *Ibid.,* April 9, 1934. Thomas said that Burton K. Wheeler endorsed the nationalization amendment. Another silver senator, Democrat James P. Pope of Idaho, said that the nationalization of all silver stocks was too drastic a proposal. Nationalization meant that speculatively held silver stocks would be turned over to the government at a profit. It also gave silver equal treatment with gold by the elimination of private hoards.

13. Pittman to Morgenthau, April 13, 1934, Pittman Papers, box 142, Government Departments folder.

14. U.S., Congress, Senate, Committee on Agriculture and Forestry, *Report, Encourage Sale of American Agricultural Surplus Products Abroad; To Provide Payment Therefor in Silver, and to Provide for Purchase of Silver,* Report No. 697, 73d Cong., 2d Sess., 1934.

15. *New York Times,* April 11, 1934.

16. *Salt Lake Tribune,* April 12, 1934.   17. *Ibid.,* April 14, 1934.

18. "Confidential Conference with Senators," April 14, 1934, Roosevelt Papers, President's Secretary's File, box 37, U.S. Senate folder.

19. *Ibid.*

20. *Salt Lake Tribune,* April 15, 1934; Henry Morgenthau briefly noted

in his diary entry dictated May 1, 1934, that Roosevelt had been conciliatory on silver with the senators at that conference and it worried him. Henry Morgenthau, Jr. Diary, I, 43, Henry Morgenthau, Jr., Papers (Franklin D. Roosevelt Library, Hyde Park, New York). Hereafter cited as Morgenthau Papers. Morgenthau's diaries constitute administrative history source books as well as an account of personal experiences. Blum, *From the Morgenthau Diaries,* I, ix.

21. *Salt Lake Tribune,* April 18, 1934; *New York Times,* April 19, 1934.

22. *Salt Lake Tribune,* April 19, 20, 21, 1934.

23. *New York Times,* April 22, 1934.

24. *Salt Lake Tribune,* April 22, 1934. The *Tribune's* special correspondent reported that the senators met at King's office before this conference and they agreed to hold out for mandatory legislation during their discussion with Roosevelt.

25. *New York Times,* April 22, 1934.

26. *Salt Lake Tribune,* April 22, 1934.

27. *Ibid.,* April 24, 1934; *New York Times,* April 24, 1934.

28. Pittman to Roosevelt, April 25, 1934, Pittman Papers, box 142, Government Departments folder.

29. *New York Times,* April 24, 1934.

30. "Upham Report," April 27, 1934, Morgenthau Papers. Upham said that Smith continued to resent the treatment he had received from the Roosevelt administration during the previous session's rush for farm legislation. This explained in part his willingness to defy the president's wishes so unmistakably.

31. Blum, *From the Morgenthau Diaries,* I, 186.

32. Cooley, "Silver Politics," pp. 152–53; Schlesinger, *Coming of the New Deal,* p. 251.

33. Morgenthau Diary, I, 49, Morgenthau Papers.

34. Wallace to Roosevelt, April 28, 1934, Roosevelt Papers, POF 229, box 6.

35. Israel, pp. 109–10. While the president's story emphasized his personal reservations on the subject of silver money, Roosevelt all but notified his cabinet only three days later that he was ready to bargain with the Silver Bloc.

36. The source of Pittman's plan is unclear. In a letter to Francis H. Brownell, Pittman acknowledged the executive's advocacy of such a plan. "I have doubts with regard to the plan for a dual metallic base" Pittman told him, because the Congress would not allow silver to be treated as a commodity. Pittman to Brownell, November 25, 1933, Pittman Papers, box 140, "B" folder. Late in 1933, to mention another possible source, James P. Warburg had begun to advocate "a limited optional use of silver by the various central banks in calculating their metallic reserves against outstanding note issues." Warburg, *Long Road Home,* p. 151. This suggestion became public as the result of an exchange of letters between Warburg and Borah. Warburg has said that "in spite of its technical nature, the exchange of letters . . . aroused considerable public discussion."

37. "Upham Report," April 27, 1934, Morgenthau Papers.

38. *New York Times,* May 2, 1934.

39. Pittman discussed it with both Morgenthau and Oliphant. Pittman to Morgenthau, February 16, 1934, Roosevelt Papers, POF 229, box 5; Israel, p. 104.

40. Pittman to Roosevelt, April 25, 1934, Pittman Papers, box 142, Government Departments folder.

41. U.S., *Congressional Record,* 73d Cong., 2d Sess., 1934, LXXVIII, Part 2 (May 2, 1934), 7909–10; *New York Times,* May 3, 1934.

42. *Salt Lake Tribune,* May 5, 1934. After this meeting, the barter idea was not mentioned.

43. *Ibid.,* May 6, 1934. Thereafter, Huey Long and Thomas combined to block the Glass bill until the latter's demands were substantially satisfied by Roosevelt. May 8, 13, 1934; U.S., *Congressional Record,* 73d Cong., 2d Sess., 1934, LXXVIII, Part 8 (May 3, 1934), 7984–85, (May 12, 1934), 8717–18.

44. *Salt Lake Tribune,* May 9, 10, 12, 1934; Everest, *Morgenthau, The New Deal, and Silver,* p. 43.

45. White to *Nevada State Journal* (Reno), May 16, 1934, Pittman Papers, box 145, Newspapers folder; *Salt Lake Tribune,* May 16, 1934. The senators talked with reporters at length after their final meeting with Roosevelt.

46. "Upham Report," May 23, 1934, Morgenthau Papers. Upham's May 18, 1934, report to Morgenthau also mentions that these senators were unhappy with the new silver purchase bill.

47. Borah to Fiesinger, May 26, 1934, Borah Papers, box 374, Silver folder.

48. Thomas to Robinson, June 2, 1934, E. Thomas Papers, box "R–S," 73d Congress file; *Salt Lake Tribune,* June 2, 1934.

49. Robinson to Thomas, June 3, 1934, E. Thomas Papers, box "R–S," 73d Congress file.

50. Blum, *From the Morgenthau Diaries,* I, 187.

51. Pittman to Roosevelt, June 8, 1934, Pittman Papers, box 142, Government Departments folder. Pittman stressed the obvious fact that American speculators would simply shift their transactions to the silver market in London.

52. Rosenman (ed.), *Public Papers,* III, 253.

53. U.S., *Congressional Record,* 73d Cong., 2d Sess., 1934, LXXVIII, Part 9 (May 23, 1934), 9427; (May 31, 1934), 10134–35; Cooley, "Silver Politics," pp. 154–61.

54. U.S., *Congressional Record,* 73d Cong., 2d Sess., 1934, LXXVIII, Part 10 (June 4, 1934), 10395.

55. Pittman to Morgenthau, May 17, 1934, Pittman Papers, box 142, Government Departments folder.

56. U.S., *Congressional Record,* 73d Cong., 2d Sess., 1934, LXXVIII, Part 10 (June 11, 1934), 11059–60.

57. The act itself precisely stipulated, in excerpt, that: Be it enacted . . . the "Silver Purchase Act of 1934. . . .

"It is hereby declared to be the policy of the United States that the proportion of silver to gold in the monetary stocks of the United States should be increased, with the ultimate objective of having and maintaining, one-fourth of the monetary value of such stocks in silver.

"Whenever and so long as the proportion of silver in the stocks of gold and silver of the United States is less than one-fourth of the monetary value of such stocks, the Secretary of the Treasury is authorized and directed to purchase silver, at home or abroad . . . at such rates, at such times, and upon such terms and conditions as he may deem reasonable and most advantageous to the public interest: . . . no purchase of silver shall be made hereunder at a price in excess of the monetary value thereof: . . . no purchases of silver situated in the continental United States on May 1, 1934, shall be made hereunder at a price in excess of 50 cents a fine ounce.

"The Secretary of the Treasury is authorized and directed to issue silver certificates, . . . and such certificates shall be placed in actual circulation. . . . All silver certificates heretofore or hereafter issued shall be legal tender for all debts, public and private. . . .

"On all transfers of any interest in silver bullion, if the price for which such interest is or is to be transferred exceeds the total of the cost thereof and allowed expenses, 50 per centum [tax on] . . . the amount of such excess [shall be assessed]." U.S., *Statutes at Large,* XLVIII, Part 1, Public Law No. 438 (March, 1933, to June, 1934), 1178–81.

58. "When the Act was passed, 1,200,000 ounces of silver would have met the requirement." Blum, *From the Morgenthau Diaries,* I, 188.

59. For a discussion of the monetary implications of these provisions see Johnson, *Treasury and Monetary Policy,* pp. 176–77. Johnson is perhaps the only authority on this subject to discuss it without polemics and moralistic undertones, as for example James Daniel Paris, *Monetary Policies of the United States, 1932–1938* (New York: Columbia University Press, 1938), pp. 50–56. A more recent general work coming close to Johnson's tone but of little usefulness on this point is Milton Friedman and Anna Jacobson Schwartz, *A Monetary History of the United States, 1867–1960* (Princeton, New Jersey: Princeton University Press, 1963), pp. 483–85.

60. This was explicit in the act: "The Secretary of the Treasury is authorized, with the approval of the President, to investigate, regulate, or prohibit, by means of licenses or otherwise, the acquisition, importation, exportation or transportation of silver and of contracts and other arrangements made with respect thereto; and to require the filing of reports deemed by him reasonably necessary in connection therewith. Whoever willfully violates . . . shall . . . be fined . . . $10,000 or . . . [be] imprisoned . . . or both. . . .

"On every . . . transfer there shall be made and delivered by the transferor to the transferee a memorandum to which there shall be affixed lawful stamps in value equal to the tax thereon. Every such memorandum shall show the date thereof, the names and addresses of the transferor and transferee, the interest in silver bullion to which it refers, the price for which such interest is or is to be transferred, and the cost thereof and the allowed expenses. Any person . . . who is a party . . . with intent to evade . . . shall be deemed guilty of a misdemeanor, and . . . shall pay . . . $1,000 or be imprisoned not more than six months or both." U.S., *Statutes at Large,* XLVIII, Part 1, Public Law No. 438 (March, 1933, to June, 1934), 1179.

61. White to *Nevada State Journal,* June 11, 1934, Pittman Papers, box 145, Newspaper folder.

62. Borah to Rockwell, June 12, 1934, Borah Papers, box 374. Ferry, Snyder and Cook each approved of it. *Salt Lake Tribune,* May 23, 1934.

63. *New York Times,* August 13, 1934; Richard T. Ruetten, "Burton K. Wheeler of Montana, A Progressive between the Wars" (Department of History, University of Oregon, 1961), pp. 137–38.

64. Evans to Borah, May 26, 1934, Cannon Papers, Borah folder.

65. *Boston Evening Transcript,* June 12, 1934.

66. *New York Times,* June 15, 25, 1934.

8 The Silver Policy

THE Treasury Department's enforcement of the Silver Purchase Act of 1934 quickly became the subject of controversy. Elmer Thomas of Oklahoma and Patrick A. McCarran of Nevada became persistent critics of the secretary, Henry Morgenthau, Jr., while Key Pittman of Nevada led the remaining members of the Silver Bloc in his defense. Pittman frequently consulted with Morgenthau about his colleagues' complaints that the Treasury's purchases were too small and that the prices it paid were too low to achieve congressional aims. They also discussed the monetary difficulties created in China by the silver program.

The initial conflict over administration of the act arose less than two months after its adoption. Early in August, 1934, Thomas and McCarran complained to reporters about the Treasury's delay in beginning substantial purchases.[1] Their criticisms were justified. While the secretary vacationed during July, his subordinates had ignored instructions to buy silver on the world market. Upon returning to Washington, Morgenthau personally started a buying campaign which quickly pushed prices up to fifty cents per ounce.[2]

The senators were pacified by rising prices and the resulting nationalization of all silver stocks. Roosevelt and Morgenthau had perviously decided to nationalize whenever prices reached fifty cents per ounce, and on August 9, the secretary issued the president's proclamation.[3] Elmer Thomas, who sponsored the provision, assumed that the result would be a substantial expansion of the circulating currency. He did not know that Morgenthau planned to retire other types of paper currency in amounts equal to the silver certificates issued by the Treasury.[4] Apparently the president also was unaware of this. He desired, according to Morgenthau, to "keep us from being criticized by Senator Thomas that we were simply using the new silver certificates to take the place of worn out certificates which are being returned to us."[5] Roosevelt even suggested that they be issued at the construction site for the Boulder Dam in Nevada "to dramatize the use of this new silver money."[6] Despite the president's intentions, Morgenthau continued his policy of limiting the supply of money.[7]

The continuing absence of pressure from the Silver Bloc allowed Roosevelt and the secretary to strive for stable silver prices. In a memorandum dated December 17, 1934, they authorized the Treasury to buy the metal from any source at a price of fifty-five cents per ounce or less. They also agreed that it should "not permit the general or world market price of silver to fall substantially below 55 cents an ounce."[8] Apparently, they believed that since Senators Pittman, Wheeler, and King had been easily reelected, they could relax pressure on the issue of prices. While this impression was partly correct, McCarran and Thomas refused to agree.

The senator from Oklahoma repudiated the Treasury's policies limiting new silver currency and stabilizing prices. He urged its officials to speed purchases on the world market, assuming that this would hasten monetary expansion. On January 16, 1935, Thomas hosted a National Monetary Conference held in Washington to highlight demands for increased money circulation. It adopted resolutions favoring legislation to create a central bank; to end the dollar's fixed relationship with gold; to remonetize silver; and to issue "non-interest bearing legal tender notes."[9] Although the conference endorsed several inflationary actions, it emphasized increased silver money circulation. Thomas told George W. Malone, chairman of the Western States Silver Committee and the Republican defeated by Key Pittman in the recent elections, that:

> All through the conference, both in and out of session, we discovered that practically everyone thought that we could

138

secure our objective better through the use of silver than through any other means; . . . a drive will be made real soon to make use of more silver in our monetary system.[10]

Thomas received little encouragement from the leading silver senators. He sought in vain to persuade Wheeler to place his remonetization bill "up for a hearing and action at an early date." Thomas suggested to Malone that "your group should have someone here to assist us and to keep the senators from the so-called silver states interested in the proceedings."[11] Key Pittman explained his reluctance to assist Thomas, and his attitude probably was shared by the other senators, except for McCarran, from the mining states. Referring to the compulsory issuance of silver certificates, Pittman told Thomas that he should present the matter to the president because he could not get a majority vote favoring the proposal in the Senate.[12]

The silverite from Oklahoma proceeded despite the indifference of his western colleagues. He wrote the president to request swift action, linking his suggestions on monetary inflation with funding of the $4.8 billion Work Relief bill then pending in the Senate. Thomas proposed (1) to issue silver certificates against all silver bullion at its monetary value, $1.29 per ounce; (2) to place all such certificates in circulation immediately in payment of the government's obligations; (3) to keep them in constant circulation; (4) to buy silver at the rate of fifty million ounces per month; (5) to authorize the Treasury to exchange gold for silver; and (6) to authorize it to accept both metals in payment of sums owing to the United States.[13] Thomas' enthusiasm apparently influenced Roosevelt. A few days after receiving Thomas' letter, he apologetically asked for information about issuing more money in a confidential memorandum to Henry Morgenthau.

Is there anything to prevent us from taking all of the seigniorage we have received on silver purchased and coin it into fifty cent pieces and dollars and use it to pay a part, if only a small one, of the work relief costs. This sounds like Senator Thomas but I would like to know what authority the law gives us.[14]

139

Excepting McCarran, Thomas failed to interest the western senators in promoting greater circulation for silver certificates. They were almost exclusively concerned with the Treasury's purchases of silver and the prices paid. By mid-April, 1935, moreover, the senators could justify their acceptance of Morgenthau's procedures. The price of silver had risen to over sixty cents per ounce because of speculative withholding of stocks from the world market.[15]

Criticism of Treasury procedures intensified conflicts within the Silver Bloc, especially between Pittman and McCarran.[16] Because McCarran sought maximum aid for the mining industry, he introduced in April an amendment to the Silver Purchase Act. He proposed to abolish the tax of 50 percent on all profits from the transfer of silver, to terminate the Treasury's authority to license all domestic transactions in the metal, and to withdraw the president's power to nationalize domestic stocks.[17]

While introducing his proposal, McCarran mentioned having asked Secretary Morgenthau certain questions about the silver program. These queries indicated that McCarran would not be satisfied until the world market price reached $1.29 per ounce. One week later Pittman told his colleagues, without mentioning the junior senator from Nevada, that he was thoroughly pleased with all phases of the administration's policy on silver. He added, however,

> From a selfish standpoint, as a Senator who represents a silver mining state, I should have been happy to see the price run up to $1.29 an ounce. . . . It probably would have doubled the prosperity we are now enjoying in mining; but . . ., to speak as a Senator of the whole United States, . . . I am compelled to approve the course [taken by] the President of the United States.[18]

By the end of April, a series of events culminated in a new understanding between the moderate silver senators and Secretary Morgenthau. The initial action involved an increase in the price for newly mined silver. The Treasury had agreed to buy at a price at least equal to that on the world market. On April 10, its price barely exceeded the world figure. That day Pittman sent a lengthy review of the purchasing policy to Roosevelt, praising his efforts on behalf of the white metal. Also, the senator suggested increasing the domestic price above sixty-four and one half cents per ounce by reducing the seigniorage from 50 to 25 percent. That tax "stimulated efforts upon the part of some congressmen," Pittman warned, "to insist upon new legislation." The following day, however, the president issued a proclamation lowering the seigniorage to 45 percent, resulting in a price of seventy-one cents per ounce for silver produced in the United States.[19]

Following the domestic price increase, the world market responded with a sharp rise. The senators were pleased but officials at the Treasury worried about a speculative boom. General Counsel Herman Oliphant noted in his diary on April 12 that "silver prices are skyrocketing," and three days later he said that Morgenthau's "loss of control of the silver market was causing a dangerous situation."[20]

Rising prices on the world market prompted a second increase in the price for newly produced silver. The former reached seventy cents per ounce on April 24, but Roosevelt and Morgenthau decided to do nothing and say nothing unless "the pressure from the [Capitol] Hill became too great." According to Oliphant, an unexpected event cancelled this resolve. He recorded that Charles Gridley, a reliable newspaper reporter, had been "in his cups" that day and had written a story saying that "the Treasury Department would hereafter buy newly mined silver only at the [world] market" price on the day of the purchase. "Key Pittman went wild and called me, mad as a hornet," Oliphant wrote, and the latter called Morgenthau, who called the president. Later that evening, Roosevelt signed a new proclamation reducing the seigniorage to 40 percent, which raised the domestic price to seventy-seven and one half cents per ounce.[21] This mollified the senator, although the price was less than he had requested.[22]

The world price soared again the following day, but this led to a turnabout in Treasury procedures. Not only were its officials upset by rapid increases, the silver senators were concerned that speculators might trigger a break in the market which would immediately bring severe criticism upon the Bloc. Excluding Thomas and McCarran, they were satisfied and willing to compromise. Senator King expressed the majority view, after the two dissidents had objected to actions by the Treasury, when he told Morgenthau: "I don't know what in the devil's getting the matter with those fellows. We—the President and you did such magnificent work and gave us that Silver Bill. . . . I don't understand it at all."[23]

The senators and the administration reached a new understanding in a conference at Secretary Morgenthau's office late in the morning of April 26, 1935. Earlier that day, Morgenthau had learned that Roosevelt was unconcerned about the possible effect of silver prices on the 1936 election. The president had approved a bid of only seventy-five cents per ounce on the world market, a figure lower than the domestic price.[24] The secretary met with Senators Borah, King, Adams, and Wheeler, a group selected during a telephone conversation between Pittman and Morgenthau. They included Wheeler after Pittman insisted: "You'd better have Wheeler down there if you're going to do anything peculiar."[25] Apparently Pittman had agreed in advance, perhaps with the president, to a policy change. Equally indicative, Pittman had excluded both Thomas and McCarran from this conference.

Two accounts were kept of Morgenthau's meeting with the Silver Bloc. Herman Oliphant summarized in his diary the viewpoints expressed and the principal decision, while Morgenthau recorded the outcome and bits of the conversation. The purpose was to set the Treasury's price for newly mined silver. Oliphant noted:

After Henry recited the dangerous speculative situation, he suggested we might raise the price for newly-mined silver five per cent at a time, go to $1.00 at once, or go to $1.29 immediately. King was emphatic that the speculators should be squeezed. The others favored going to $1.29. Borah was fairest of all. He said he approved the way the matter had been handled and would approve whatever the Secretary decided. The final agreement was to do nothing for three or four days.[26]

Morgenthau emphasized that Pittman agreed on the harmful effect of speculation. "The only thing that will stop speculation is to give the speculators a loss," he told the group after Morgenthau had introduced the subject. Also, he objected to raising the price to $1.29, as did Senator King, while the others, Borah, Wheeler, and Adams, favored it. When further discussion produced objections to each alternative, Pittman said, "I think you ought to sit tight and do nothing and wait four or five days." Wheeler agreed, Borah had no objection, Adams said nothing, and Morgenthau said that he would wait.[27]

The senators' tolerance permitted the secretary to use procedures not authorized in the Silver Purchase Act. He sold small amounts of the metal, bringing the world price down to below seventy-five cents per ounce within the following three weeks. Through alternating purchases and sales, Morgenthau held the price at that point for several months. On May 15, the secretary formally apprised Pittman of the new procedures and the results. The senator expressed his complete satisfaction.[28] Thereafter, the Treasury's price for newly mined silver remained at 77.57 cents, and world prices stayed below that figure.

The Treasury Department's new procedures irritated McCarran and Thomas. The latter soon publicized his objection. On a day when world market prices slid five cents per ounce, Thomas complained to his colleagues that lower prices meant the Treasury had ignored the will of the Congress expressed in the Silver Purchase Act. His interest in the matter was strong, he said, because "the price of cotton follows the price of silver."[29]

Shortly thereafter, McCarran revealed publicly his growing displeasure. Early in June, he announced a meeting of the Silver Bloc to discuss the Treasury's management of its mandate. Because of recent sales, McCarran wondered if Morgenthau pursued the silver policy as enthusiastically as he had pledged a year earlier.[30] Also, the senator requested in writing all the facts on recent purchases and sales, explaining why prices had "strangely"

143

fallen from their April high of eighty-one cents per ounce.[31] Morgenthau accepted McCarran's challenge, answering in a straight-forward manner without apology. After changing a reply drafted by Oliphant to suit his own tastes, Morgenthau called Key Pittman, who hurried over to dictate several blunt, strongly worded paragraphs, but Morgenthau later decided to delete these recriminations. The final draft contained a detailed résumé of the silver policy. With respect to prices, Morgenthau said that he approved the end of speculative "manipulations" because "the disappearance of this unhealthy condition and influence has been a wholesome development."[32]

McCarran forged ahead. His gathering for those senators interested in the "welfare and stabilization of silver as money" met on the afternoon of June 19 at the Senate Office Building.[33] This meeting revealed a formal split in the Bloc. McCarran underscored that fact by announcing that his group, which included Thomas and Smith of South Carolina, planned to discuss matters with the secretary of the Treasury.[34] After the latter heard of this, he called Pittman, who advised him that "if you call in those . . . fellows and you don't take everything they say down in shorthand, they're going to come back and say what they please to the President."[35] Morgenthau also talked with King about the imminent visit of McCarran's group, asking him "how it would be" if he, King, and other moderates were invited over at the same time. King laughed and said, "I don't think that they would welcome that," but later he agreed to the secretary's arrangements. Morgenthau told the senator that he would say to the dissidents: "I want the senators who live in the silver states," because "[farmers] don't raise much silver in South Carolina."[36] After Morgenthau's thorough preparations, McCarran failed to request a meeting.

McCarran's splinter group urged the purchase of more silver at higher prices. In July, Thomas drafted a formal complaint, which contained numbered statements specifying the congressional intent expressed in the Silver Purchase Act. After obtaining the signatures of forty-six colleagues, Thomas sent it to the president. He included a cover letter which summarized the peti-

tion and requested that the "silver policy be carried out enthusiastically."[37] Roosevelt's reply emphasized that he supported his
secretary of the Treasury and that the measure was being "carried
out vigorously and in good faith."[38]

The complaints were partly justified. Not only had prices for
silver fallen below seventy cents per ounce, but monthly purchases during the first half of 1935 averaged nearly 20 percent
less than during the preceding five months.[39] Morgenthau circum-
vented this criticism by claiming that the total acquisitions—
domestic, nationalized, and world market—exceeded forty-two
million ounces a month. While this rebuttal was accurate, it did
not conceal the fact of changes in the Treasury's procedures.[40]

Following the failure of individual and group protests the mili-
tant senators devised a legislative offensive in two parts. The first
was McCarran's proposal introduced earlier to eliminate the tax
on profits from silver transactions. The second was a request by
Thomas for a Senate investigation of the Treasury's administration of its mandate to purchase the white metal. These measures
were offered almost simultaneously late in that session of the
Congress.

On August 15, 1935, McCarran offered his amendment to the
Silver Purchase Act as a rider to a pending appropriations bill.
Previously, the Agriculture committee reported the amendment
favorably at the behest of Thomas and Smith of South Carolina.[41]
The administration's supporters in the Senate acquiesced, and it
was adopted without a roll call.[42] This resulted from an earlier
agreement between Majority Leader Robinson and Morgenthau,
who had said that the McCarran amendment "doesn't bother
me."[43] However, the House of Representatives later ruled the
amendment out of order because of its right to initiate all revenue
legislation.[44]

Morgenthau accepted McCarran's proposal to forestall the investigation sought by Thomas. Apparently, the secretary selected
the lesser of two evils. He had told Robinson that Thomas could
be stopped through the intercession of George Le Blanc, a spec-
ulator who dabbled in the silver market. He would favor elimination of the 50 percent tax on profits proposed by McCarran, and

he would gain nothing from inquiry into the Treasury's purchases of silver.[45]

With Pittman's assistance, Morgenthau devised a strategy to prevent an investigation. After gaining Robinson's approval and cooperation, the secretary telephoned Le Blanc, who agreed to persuade Thomas to postpone his request. Later, in a return call, Le Blanc said Thomas would delay his resolution until the following day.[46] Meanwhile, Pittman won approval for a measure creating a Senate Special Silver Committee authorized to investigate the Treasury's execution of the Silver Purchase Act.[47] Pittman's action assured his jurisdiction over any examination of the Treasury's activities relevant to the act, and it prevented Thomas from launching his own probe. The resolution he introduced the following day was later ruled out of order.[48] Pittman then invited Thomas to serve on the special committee.

Pittman's committee failed to conduct an inquiry. On August 26, it held a brief, unannounced meeting to indicate that an investigation would begin at Salt Lake City sometime in October. Thomas learned of this in a letter from Pittman's assistant.[49] In reply, he expressed hope that he would be notified in time to attend the session in Utah.[50] However, Pittman later cancelled that meeting.

The president objected to the proposed investigation. On August 26, he told Senator King that he was "quite satisfied" with the silver program and he would resist demands from dissenting senators. King relayed this information to reporters, mentioning that, as a member of the special committee, he did not believe it would recommend any changes.[51]

Despite the general satisfaction, a major revision in the Treasury's procedures occurred later that year because of altered circumstances in the domestic and foreign scene. At home, radical strength waned rapidly in 1935 as urban discontent diminished and rural agitation faded away. Moreover, the death that September of Senator Huey Long removed the potential leader of a third party in the forthcoming presidential campaign. Roosevelt had not discounted that possibility.[52] While unrest subsided in the

West and the South, matters became more complex in China due in part to its export of silver to the United States.

During 1934 and 1935, the national government of China had repeatedly warned Washington that it might eventually be forced to abandon the silver standard. The first of these warnings had come on October 1, 1934, triggering a negative reaction from Key Pittman. In a letter to the president, he said that this "ultimatum" should be ignored since the Chinese could not afford gold nor abandon silver because of their ancient traditions.[53] The senator had lost touch with events in Asia; his view reflected its situation more than a year earlier when he had taked with T. V. Soong. Pittman soon learned about changing opinion there. A letter from Victor S. Clark, an American economist then visiting Shanghai, provided a personal and well-informed appraisal of the current impact in 1934 of American silver policies on China.

Our silver policy, so far as it has influenced international silver prices, is unpopular here. It is held responsible for the decline in foreign trade and the general business recession of the past eight or ten months. I have not been here long enough . . . to judge how far the present unsatisfactory status of business is attributable to that particular cause. I fancy several factors are at work. Nevertheless, there has been a great draining of silver from the country into Shanghai and other ports, with a corresponding shrinkage in the purchasing power of the country people.[54]

Pittman's attitude toward China indicated a feeling widely prevalent at that time. Most Americans and their elected representatives concentrated upon the immediate need to bring about domestic recovery, asserting that all other considerations must be secondary. The fact that an election campaign was then in progress made the Chinese declaration all the more unpopular.

Moreover, the senators refused to consider such criticism before the policy had received a full trial. The president accepted their view and vetoed the Treasury Department's suggestion that T. V. Soong be invited to Washington for discussions.[55] Pittman summed up his attitude on such foreign protests in a letter to Herman Oliphant: "I do not believe that we can afford to interfere with our policy at the present time by reason of the necessity of foreign countries to alter their own monetary systems."[56]

Indeed, the president believed that the American policy helped China in the long run. In a memorandum to Secretary Morgenthau, dated December 4, 1934, he said:

I am inclined to believe that the "money changers" are wrong and that it is better to hasten the crisis in China—to compel the Chinese people more and more to stand on their own feet without complete dependence on Japan and Europe —than it is to compromise with a situation which is economically unsound and which compromise will mean the continuation of an unsound position for a generation to come.[57]

Thus, the two political leaders agreed. Roosevelt thought that China's financial house needed a thorough reordering rather than a mere palliative, while Pittman rejected the pleas from that nation as inconsistent with American policy.

During most of 1935, domestic considerations outweighed objections from abroad. On July 11, Morgenthau discussed China's problem with Pittman, telling him of an appeal by General Chiang Kai-shek for a change in American policy. The general had insisted that the high price for silver (then sixty-five cents per ounce) encouraged smuggling, helped Japan, and might force China off the silver standard. In reaction, Morgenthau proposed a set price for purchases on the world market. This would aid Chinese business interests and ease pressure on the generalissimo. Pittman said that while such a step might help China, he must advise against it because Senators Thomas and McCarran were certain to raise a storm over any change in policy. During the following month, however, Morgenthau adopted a standard bid of 65.37 cents per ounce on the world market. This offer remained unchanged until late that year.[58]

When China abandoned a silver standard, the president lost interest in sustaining the world market for the metal. Morgenthau informed him of China's new policy on November 4, 1935, mentioning also that Pittman had told the press that due to China's action silver prices would rise to $1.29 within eighteen months. The secretary recorded Roosevelt's reply.

Much to my surprise, the President's response to this information was "Key Pittman is cock-eyed." I gather from this that the President is less interested in putting up the price of silver than he used to be. This is the first indication that I have had along these lines.[59]

Several days later, on November 9, the president discussed lowering the Treasury's bid on the world market with Morgenthau and Oliphant. They decided against such a move at that time.[60]

The president's subsequent decision to lower the Treasury's bid resulted from a sudden flood of silver into the world market. Early in December, British officials at Hong Kong nationalized silver within the colony and immediately began selling it in large quantities. Observers expected China to follow suit, prompting Morgenthau to confer with Roosevelt. On December 7, they decided to begin lowering the world price.[61]

Morgenthau did not advise the senators. The secretary decided, after first consulting with the president, that "after we acted, if the silver Senators wanted to know what we were doing, I would ask Key Pittman to call a meeting of his [special] committee to meet with me."[62] However, the senators readily accepted the change. On December 10, Pittman asked Morgenthau if the domestic price would be changed; he said no, and the former quickly replied, "I do not care what you do with the world price as long as you leave the domestic price alone."[63] So ended the Silver Bloc's drive to restore the international monetary status and value of the white metal.

Morgenthau gradually lowered his bid on the world market despite objections by Senator Thomas. On December 11, 1935, the price declined from sixty-five to sixty-one cents per ounce; the senator dissented. He demanded a "concerted buying program until silver reaches $1.29 an ounce where it should be stabilized." He also said that the Treasury should either put the price up or cease buying entirely. The latter course would bring a sharp break in prices. A Chinese source announced that a sudden drop would be as harmful to Chinese interests as were the past upward movements.[64] Morgenthau adopted a middle course: during the following forty days, he gradually lowered the Treasury's bid to forty-five cents. He sought to put the silver market down to "where the world will support the price for whatever [is] the intrinsic value of silver."[65] Late in December, Thomas goaded Pittman with a telegraphed reminder that "your cooperation in carrying out our adopted silver policy will be appreciated."[66] If Thomas believed he could stir the senator, he was quickly disappointed. "There are monetary and exchange factors which justify the present course," Pittman publicly remarked one week later; "I am satisfied that Secretary Morgenthau is conducting the purchase program satisfactorily."[67]

The American decision to lower prices followed closely upon China's decision to abandon silver in an effort to ward off an inevitable economic disaster. Early in 1936, W. Y. Lin, a Chinese monetary specialist residing in Shanghai, presented his interpretation.

> In view of the growing adverse balance of international payments and in the absence of a continued inflow of foreign capital, the external drain of the precious metals was not at all surprising. . . . The alarming external drain of silver was an inevitable consequence of the unfavorable turn in China's balance of payments and it was merely aggravated by the American Silver Policy. . . .[68]

Dickenson H. Leavens, an American mathematician, writing somewhat earlier at Cambridge, Massachusetts, took a less charitable view of American culpability. While conceding that other factors were involved, he was disheartened that China's troubles had been "accentuated by a professedly friendly nation, which has taken action embarrassing to China, merely for the sake of satisfying certain economically insignificant but politically important interests at home."[69]

The degree of American responsibility for China's monetary troubles was not precisely measurable, but Pittman and Morgenthau did not ignore its existence. The former was not pleased with the situation and he granted his own responsibility, at least by implication. On the evening of January 2, 1936, the senator told the secretary, no doubt sadly, that "the Silver Act was never intended to force the other countries off silver."[70] Morgenthau had expressed the same frustration earlier when he told a reporter for the *Wall Street Journal* that American policy had aided the Japanese, who were "bleeding China white" by draining away that nation's silver and selling the metal to the United States.[71]

The silver purchase program became a domestic issue. Morgenthau recorded his concern at that time. It was "the only monetary fiscal policy that I cannot explain or justify [to the public] . . ., but if I could expose it to the world now it will save us much grief during the coming campaign."[72] If the president shared the secretary's qualms it was not noted, but Blum has said that Roosevelt later referred to it jokingly as "the forbidden subject."[73]

Published comment on the silver policy had grown increasingly critical. The editors of the *New York Times,* for example, were alarmed by mid-1935 over the massive purchases of the metal. In an editorial entitled "The Silver Fantasy," they were incredulous. "That the future of our currency should be deeply involved in an effort to benefit by the present means so small an industry would be unbelievable if it were not actually happening."[74] Early the following year, moreover, Professor Ray B. Westerfield of Yale published a book entitled *Our Silver Debacle.* The target of his bitter criticism was not only the Silver Bloc, but the president, because he "had made inflation a key policy of his administration." According to Westerfield, Roosevelt

had promised to help the farmer and the debtor by any and every inflationary device if necessary. Silver speculators justifiably expected that he would do as well by silver as he did by gold. When the head of the nation adopts the policy of subsidizing special classes, it is difficult to stop short and deny highly organized, politically active minorities their slice of the public bacon![75]

In succeeding years, negative opinions on the buying of both foreign and domestic silver became steadily more vehement. One popular writer asserted that the New Deal seemed determined to crucify the nation on a "cross of silver."[76] Another complained that the Treasury had in its vaults three billion ounces of silver which it could "neither sell, use, coin, nor give away."[77] Sylvia F. Porter later claimed, in an article titled "Uncle Sam's Silver Scandal," that the "key to America's Alice-in-wonderland silver folly lies in two words—politics and depression." She explained the matter very simply: "the Senate's 'silver bloc' of 14 men, one of the strongest political groups ever formed, has exploited hard times to promote the metal."[78]

Writers for more scholarly audiences used similar tones. Herbert M. Bratter, an authority on silver as a commodity, found no justification for the Silver Purchase Act of 1934. Four years after its adoption, he wrote:

If the Act had been merely futile it would have been bad enough. . . . The mandatory feature of the Act as regulated by the original gentlemen's agreement between the silver bloc and the administration entailed inevitable grief, both diplomatic and political. This was not a matter for experiment to verify; it was an inescapable truth which had been thoroughly revealed long before the Act's passage.[79]

Later, Arthur M. Schlesinger, Jr., wrote that the silver industry had extorted nearly a billion and a half dollars from the federal government in the fifteen years after 1934. He also contended that "no legislation passed in New Deal years had less excuse."[80]

Neither of the primary objectives of the Silver Purchase Act were achieved. Prices on the world market returned to the level of forty-five cents per ounce early in 1936 and thereafter the goal of $1.29 was forgotten. The Treasury Department also failed to attain the balance of metallic reserves—one-fourth silver to three-fourths gold—specified in the measure. Gold stocks increased so substantially after 1934 that more than twice as much silver was needed to establish that proportion than originally contemplated. The Treasury's purchases absorbed huge quantities of the metal however, assuring that when industrial demand increased, prices might also rise.[81] In the meantime, American policy provided a market for producers and for the foreign governments that demonetized their stocks. In summary, the act resulted in a form of relief to industrial and governmental holders of the metal, but it otherwise failed to achieve its proponents' objectives.[82] To be sure, it was not the measure but the Treasury's policies which prevented a substantial increase in the quantity of money in circulation.[83]

Although the Silver Purchase Act was anathematized after 1935, the western senators ignored world prices and carefully guarded the domestic subsidy. The price for newly mined silver remained at seventy-seven and one-half cents per ounce until December 31, 1937, when the president reduced it to sixty-four and one-half cents.[84] A year and a half later, the Congress fixed the price by statute at seventy-one cents per ounce.[85] This action ended the president's responsibility but retained monetary status for bullion purchased under the program. While its effect on the supply of money was minimal, domestic industry received more than $160 million by June of 1938 through exchanging the metal for silver certificates.[86] Producers welcomed this assistance from Washington both during and after the decade of depression.[87]

The subsidy particularly benefited the West. The fixed price for domestic output and low costs of production during the thirties guaranteed profitable operation for marginal mines. This permitted smaller companies to survive the depression and induced them to reopen shafts closed since the early twenties. The subsidy provided employment in the remote mining camps and sustained communities otherwise bereft of cash income and alternative occupations.[88] Viewed as relief to thousands of miners and their families otherwise unable to escape the scourge of idleness and want, the domestic silver policy was a wise investment in the future of a troubled land. Franklin D. Roosevelt so conceived his New Deal for the American people.

1. *New York Times,* August 2, 1934.
2. Blum, *From the Morgenthau Diaries,* I, 189–90, 194. From August to December, 1934, purchases averaged twenty-four million ounces a month, and the total purchases during the first eleven months, July, 1934, through May, 1935, were 283 million ounces.

3. Morgenthau Diary, II, 14, Morgenthau Papers.

4. Blum, *From the Morgenthau Diaries,* I, 188–89. During the year ending June, 1935, the monetary stock rose only 11 percent and circulation per capita only 3 percent.

5. Morgenthau Diary, II, 18.

6. *Ibid.* Roosevelt's suggestion may have been intended to aid Pittman's campaign for reelection. Pittman to Roosevelt, August 10, 1934, Roosevelt Papers, PPF 745.

7. Morgenthau Diary, II, 61. Certificates were issued only to meet the costs of the purchases. The seigniorage was not monetized.

8. *Ibid.,* p. 293.

9. Thomas to Roosevelt, January 18, 1935, Roosevelt Papers, POF 229, box 8.

10. Thomas to Malone, January 19, 1935, E. Thomas Papers, box "S–T," 74th Congress file. Thomas expected cooperation from Wheeler in his drive, but not from "such pseudo-silver Senators as Senator King, Pittman and others, yet I am not willing to relax my efforts." Thomas to John Janney, February 11, 1935, box 460, Money—currency file.

11. *Ibid.* The Oklahoma senator also failed to get assistance from Senator Borah. Thomas to Borah, December 18, 1934, Borah Papers, box 374, Silver folder.

12. Pittman to Thomas, February 28, 1935, E. Thomas Papers, box "S," 74th Congress file.

13. Thomas to Roosevelt, March 8, 1935, Roosevelt Papers, POF 229, box 8.

14. Roosevelt to Morgenthau, April 16, 1935, Roosevelt Papers, POF 229, box 8.

15. Leavens, *Silver Money,* p. 356. See the chart titled: "Monthly High and Low Price of Silver, 1933–1938."

16. They continued their duel for control of Nevada's Democratic party. Pittman thought McCarran guilty of encouraging opposition to him in the 1934 campaign. Israel, p. 111.

17. U.S., *Congressional Record,* 74th Cong., 1st Sess., 1935, LXXIX, Part 5 (April 4, 1935), 4983. See S. 2507.

18. *Ibid.* (April 11, 1935), p. 5404.

19. Pittman to Roosevelt, April 10, 1935, Pittman Papers, box 142, Government Departments folder; U.S., *Statutes at Large,* XLIX, Part 2, Proclamation No. 2124, 3445; Morgenthau Diary, IV, 178.

20. Oliphant to Morgenthau, August 19, 1935, Morgenthau Papers, box 216, Oliphant, Confidential file. The letter included excerpts from Oliphant's diary.

21. *Ibid.;* U.S., *Statutes at Large,* XLIX, Part 2, Proclamation No. 2125, 3445–46.

22. Pittman to Roosevelt, April 23, 1935, Pittman Papers, box 142, Government Departments folder. Pittman suggested that only 35 percent be retained for seigniorage.

23. Morgenthau Diary, VIII, 8B. Excerpt from an entry for June 19, 1935.

24. *Ibid.,* pp. 28–29. 25. *Ibid.,* p. 29A.

26. Oliphant to Morgenthau, August 19, 1935, Morgenthau Papers, box 216, Oliphant, Confidential file. Excerpt is from an entry in Oliphant's diary dated April 26, 1935.

27. Morgenthau Diary, V, 30–31. Morgenthau's remarks as recorded in Oliphant's diary suggest that the former favored raising the price to $1.29, the

course advocated by the latter. Oliphant to Morgenthau, August 29, 1935, Morgenthau Papers, box 216, Oliphant Confidential file.

28. Morgenthau Diary, V, 90. Blum, *From the Morgenthau Diaries,* I, 193. Earlier, King expressed the same feeling. Morgenthau Diary, V, 60 B.

29. U.S., *Congressional Record,* 74th Cong., 1st Sess., 1935, LXXIX, Part 6 (May 2, 1935), 6771.

30. *New York Times,* June 9, 1935.

31. Morgenthau to McCarran, June 11, 1935, Pittman Papers, box 142, Government Departments folder. McCarran's leading questions were repeated in Morgenthau's reply.

32. Morgenthau Diary, VI, 50–56.

33. McCarran to Elmer Thomas, June 18, 1935, E. Thomas Papers, box 303, Silver file.

34. Morgenthau Diary, VII, 5. Entry of June 18, 1935.

35. *Ibid.,* p. 6.   36. *Ibid.,* pp. 8A, 8B.

37. Thomas to Roosevelt, July 22, 1935, Roosevelt Papers, POF 229, box 9.

38. Roosevelt to Gentlemen, July 25, 1935, Roosevelt Papers, POF 229, box 9.

39. Morgenthau Diary, VII, 183. From January to July, 1935, purchases averaged twenty million ounces a month.

40. *Ibid.,* p. 56.

41. U.S., Congress, Senate, Committee on Agriculture and Forestry, *Report, Repeal of Sections 6, 7, and 8 of the Silver Purchase Act of 1934,* Report No. 1191, 74th Cong., 1st Sess., 1935, p. 1.

42. U.S., *Congressional Record,* 74th Cong., 1st Sess., 1935, LXXIX, Part 12 (August 15, 1935), 13240; Part 13 (August 24, 1935), 14627–31, 14633–34. See also Morgenthau Diary, IX, 32B, D, E, F.

43. Morgenthau Diary, IX, 32B.

44. U.S., *Congressional Record,* 74th Cong., 2d Sess., 1935, LXXX, Part 1 (January 15, 1936), 448.

45. Morgenthau Diary, IX, 32B.   46. *Ibid.,* p. 39E.

47. U.S., *Congressional Record,* 74th Cong., 1st Sess., 1935, LXXIX, Part 12 (August 14, 1935), 13198. See Senate Resolution 187.

48. *Ibid.,* p. 13243.

49. James A. White to Elmer Thomas, August 31, 1935, E. Thomas Papers, box "S–T," 74th Congress file. Pittman selected White as secretary to the Special Committee and its chief investigator. White was also a member of Pittman's senatorial staff.

50. Thomas to White, August 31, 1935, E. Thomas Papers, box "S–T," 74th Congress file.

51. *New York Times,* September 27, 1935.

52. Arthur M. Schlesinger, Jr., *The Age of Roosevelt,* III, *The Politics of Upheaval* (Boston: Houghton Mifflin Company, 1960), 341.

53. Pittman to Roosevelt, October 3, 1934, Roosevelt Papers, POF 229, box 7.

54. Clark to Pittman, October 29, 1934, Pittman Papers, box 141, "C" folder.

55. Morgenthau Diary, III, 1, 84. Pittman had stipulated that if Soong were invited, it should not be "to discuss our silver policy but rather foreign exchange problems."

56. Pittman to Oliphant, January 25, 1935, Pittman Papers, box 142, Government Departments folder.

57. Blum, *From the Morgenthau Diaries,* I, 206.

58. Morgenthau Diary, VIII, 60; Leavens, *Silver Money,* p. 290; Blum, *From the Morgenthau Diaries,* I, 195.

59. Morgenthau Diary, XI, 22. Morgenthau dictated this entry on November 6, 1935.

60. *Ibid.,* pp. 63–66.   61. *Ibid.,* XIII, 90.   62. *Ibid.,* p. 91.

63. *Ibid.,* p. 218. Entry of December 11, 1935, reporting previous day's conversation.

64. *Ibid.,* pp. 180, 182, 184.

65. *Ibid.,* p. 225. Entry of December 12, 1935.

66. Thomas to Pittman, December 19, 1935, E. Thomas Papers, box 303, Silver file. Thomas also wrote to W. Mont. Ferry saying, "if we can secure the enthusiastic cooperation of Senator Pittman and Senator King . . . , we have the power in Congress to force through any sort of necessary legislation." Thomas to Ferry, December 21, 1935, box 451, Money—conference file.

67. Morgenthau Diary, XIV, 212. Pittman's remarks were taken from the United Press News Wire of December 26, 1935. Wheeler also was satisfied. He would have done, he said, "exactly the same" had he been secretary of the Treasury. XVIII, 120.

68. Lin, *The New Monetary System of China,* p. 30. It must be noted that the author was predisposed to favor China's abandonment of the silver standard. Others, particularly foreign investors who were hurt by the change, were not so kind when referring to the responsibility borne by American policy.

69. Dickenson H. Leavens, "American Silver Policy and China," *Harvard Business Review,* XIV (Autumn, 1935), 58.

70. Morgenthau Diary, XV, 29.

71. *Ibid.,* XIII, 223. The entry is dated December 12, 1935.

72. *Ibid.,* p. 225.   73. Blum, *From the Morgenthau Diaries,* I, 199.

74. *New York Times,* August 16, 1935.

75. Ray B. Westerfield, *Our Silver Debacle* (New York: The Ronald Press, 1936), p. 62.

76. John H. Crider, "Cross of Silver," *The North American Review,* CCXLV (June, 1938), 280.

77. Herbert Corey, "The Silver Swindle," *The American Mercury,* XLVIII (September, 1939), 19.

78. Sylvia F. Porter, "Uncle Sam's Silver Scandal," *Reader's Digest,* XXXVI (May, 1940), 77.

79. Herbert M. Bratter, "The Silver Episode, II," *Journal of Political Economy,* XLVI (December, 1938), 837.

80. Schlesinger, *Coming of the New Deal,* p. 252.

81. U.S., *Annual Report of the Secretary of the Treasury . . . 1934,* pp. 120–21; *1935,* p. 136; *1936,* p. 165; *1937,* p. 172; *1938,* p. 180. For a convenient and accurate compilation of this data see Leavens, *Silver Money,* p. 273. See chart: "Silver Purchased by United States Treasury: Fiscal Years 1934 to 1938." The total amount acquired through June, 1938, was 1,711,008,259 ounces at a cost in silver certificates of $973,405,789.

82. Blum, *From the Morgenthau Diaries,* I, 199–228. The effects of the silver program after 1935 have been examined in depth from the perspective of the users of silver: see Everest, *Morgenthau, the New Deal, and Silver,* pp. 62–175.

83. Johnson, *Treasury and Monetary Policy,* pp. 192–95.

84. U.S., *Statutes at Large,* LII, Proclamation No. 2268, 1530–31.

85. *Ibid.,* LIII, Part 2, Public Law No. 165, 998–99.

86.   Leavens, *Silver Money*, p. 273. From July, 1934, through June, 1938, the Treasury acquired 219,951,173 ounces of newly-mined domestic silver at a cost in silver certificates of $163,582,031. U.S., *Annual Report of the Secretary of the Treasury* . . . *1934*, pp. 120–21; *1935*, p. 136; *1936*, p. 165; *1937*, p. 172; *1938*, p. 180.

87.   The price for newly-mined silver remained at seventy-one cents per ounce until July, 1946, when the seigniorage was reduced to 30 percent. This raised the price to ninety and one half cents per ounce. U.S., *Statutes at Large*, LX, Part 1, Public Law No. 579, 750. In 1963, the Congress repealed all silver purchase legislation. LXXVII, Part 1, Public Law No. 83–36, 54.

88.   The number of mines producing silver and gold rose from 4,069 in 1931 to 12,194 in 1935. By state, the totals in that year were: California, 2,599; Colorado, 1,712; Idaho, 1,368; Montana, 1,232; Arizona, 1,197; Nevada, 855; New Mexico, 384; Oregon, 383; and Utah, 235. U.S., Bureau of Mines, *Minerals Yearbook, 1937*, p. 126.

9 The Demise of the Silver Issue

Amidst the distressing thirties, many westerners remembered the era before World War I as a period of contentment. Frontier times were memories by then and the West enjoyed a steady growth in population and in usable resources. Although the "boom" era had passed, mining and farming remained generally profitable. The future seemed secure because the world would always need minerals and staple crops garnered from western mountains and plains.

While the nation's business community recovered after the steep post-war recession, farmers and mineowners experienced increasing financial difficulties. Prices for agricultural commodities and metals declined while production costs remained above prewar levels. The economic squeeze plagued producers of cotton, wheat, and silver during the twenties, and crushed them in the years that followed.[1] The representatives of mining and agriculture sought federal assistance to help cope with their economic dilemma.

Western senators responded to calls for aid by proclaiming the need for federal action. They held that expanding the stocks of monetary silver would ease the gold shortage, increase the money supply, and encourage the resumption of normal trade and commerce. Such action would also raise the price of silver, they asserted, thereby increasing the purchasing power of those Asian peoples who used it as their primary circulating medium and as a store of wealth. The higher price would also help the farmer, many believed, because prices for other commodities rose and fell in the white metal's wake. Finally, the senators said

159

that the issuance of silver certificates in exchange for silver bullion would provide employment in the mining industry and rescue many western communities. Whatever their merits, these arguments were eagerly received by many persons caught in the economic depression, and they provided a rationale for efforts to "do something for silver" in the thirties.

After 1932, the silver senators' drive for prompt and effective relief attracted strong support from representatives of the western, southern, and middle western agricultural regions. Their combined votes made a powerful unit in the Senate. Controlling such important committees as Finance, Agriculture, and Foreign Relations, their leaders ably forced legislation through the congressional machinery. Importantly, the senior members of this bloc had experienced the political crusades led by William Jennings Bryan. Their attitudes on the silver question were far more complex and emotional than those usually attributed to special-interest politics. They believed in arguments for the white metal and they rejected pleas from their eastern colleagues for resistance to demands by farmers, miners, and other citizens of the West.

Congressional silverites proposed mandatory programs unacceptable to the president. Senator Wheeler of Montana demanded free silver coinage at the ratio of sixteen to one with gold. Congressman Dies of Texas urged the export of agricultural surpluses in exchange for silver, and Congressman Fiesinger of Ohio proposed the purchase of fifty million ounces per month until one billion ounces had been added to the monetary system. If adopted, each of these measures would have expanded the money supply more than Roosevelt and his advisors deemed wise.

The Roosevelt administration accepted two measures that increased the stocks of monetary silver, thereby aiding the mining industry. The first was the Thomas amendment to the Agricultural Adjustment Act, which authorized the Treasury Department to exchange silver certificates for the white metal. Using this power, Roosevelt ordered the purchase of all newly mined domestic silver, thereby ratifying the Silver Agreement signed in 1933 by delegates from eight nations attending the London Economic and Monetary Conference. The second was the Silver Purchase Act of 1934, which authorized substantial purchases on the world market for the purpose of increasing prices and expanding the Treasury's stocks of silver bullion. These programs had strong support in the Congress, but the president controlled them under permissive authority enabling him to make changes in response to new conditions.

Roosevelt held the central role in developing a silver policy. While he did not publicy reject the silverites' arguments, he refused to endorse their legislative proposals. It was doubtful that he thought monetary experiments alone would raise prices for commodities. Roosevelt was consistently cautious about theoretical solutions to economic problems. He was a pragmatist; therefore, he experimented with several ideas relevant to gold and silver to ascertain their merits. The alternative to such "tinkering" was acceptance of Hoover's deflationary policies while he urgently sought to inflate prices for commodities.

The president's policies on silver were but one response to widespread demands for relief. He seemed more concerned over the public's recognition of his intentions than with the specific content of policy. Roosevelt recognized the anxieties underlying demands for increasing prices, expanding the currency, buying silver, and issuing paper money. Moreover, federal action dramatized his solicitude for individuals unable to overcome the credit deflation, particularly in the West. Roosevelt found the benefits from a subsidy to producers more significant than any monetary abuses resulting from the issue of silver certificates. This may be interpreted as a squandering of public resources to buy votes for the Democratic party, as a sensitive exercise in national leadership, or as a subtle mixture of both in undeterminable quantities.

A complex relationship united the president and the Silver Bloc. Twelve of the legislators were Democrats, and several were senior members of the Senate who supported Roosevelt's policies. In 1934, Senators Pittman, Wheeler, and King desired reelection, and the president sought a strong endorsement for his war on depression through large majorities for Democratic candidates in the congressional elections of that year. Therefore, silver legisla-

161

tion held mutual benefits. Despite this, the senators needed Roosevelt's support for their proposals more than he needed their cooperation in the Senate. Generally, they approved his measures to relieve want and to revive agriculture and industry. The president and the senators maintained effective working relations during the First New Deal.

The most influential of the silver senators were Pittman, Wheeler, and Borah. Pittman urged a subsidy, Wheeler championed remonetization, and Borah advocated an international approach. Only Pittman's goals were achieved, although the president received authority for remonetization, and American representatives participated in the monetary and economic discussions at London. Roosevelt respected Pittman's ability and his direct approach to tangible objectives. The senator's persistent efforts obtained government support for silver producers until market demand and prices returned to predepression levels.

Senator Elmer Thomas led the Farm Bloc's drive for monetary reforms. His legislative efforts relative to gold, silver, and paper currency heightened pressures upon the president to manipulate the monetary structure and to increase commodity prices. While the Roosevelt administration rarely used his audacious proposals, Thomas was a helpful and powerful ally to the Silver Bloc. He commanded the votes that made inflation an important issue in the Senate. His friendship with Father Coughlin probably increased his influence on monetary issues. While many of Thomas' ideas were ignored or rejected, Roosevelt agreed with his demands for political controls over money. The administration used these powers moderately, but their existence coincided with the trend toward economic planning at the national level.

Experiments with money disturbed many easterners, who distrusted silver-conscious western legislators. Easterners believed these senators had forced undesirable measures upon the president as the price of support for his legislative program. Some critics condemned them for pursuing, at the behest of "selfish" mining interests, goals which were potentially harmful to the nation. Those who were skeptical of the senators' motives found proof for their suspicions when China abandoned the silver standard as a result, apparently, of American purchases of the white metal.

Perhaps the most controversial aspect of the silver program was its simultaneous benefit to producers and detriment to consumers. Critics professed dismay because federal action had increased prices in the absence of legitimate demand. This seemed intolerable since they frequently did not understand that the subsidy was self-supporting, and, moreover, believed that it was a direct burden on the taxpayer. Finally, most observers were disturbed because this dubious policy created difficulties for nations with substantial amounts of silver coinage. While objectors grossly misjudged the domestic outcome, they correctly assessed the harmful international results.

Despite the unfortunate effects attributable to the silver policy, members of the Silver Bloc had exercised moderation in promoting the white metal. They only reluctantly supported independent bimetallism. They secured greater use of silver as money without causing a constant drain on the nation's stocks of monetary gold. In 1935, most of the senators agreed to eliminate speculation in the metal and to stabilize world prices. However, they were reluctant to concede the harmful effects of high prices for silver upon China's already troubled economy. The resulting flow of metal from that country to the United States confounded assumptions and confirmed the predictions of critics.

Clashing opinions on economic and monetary questions, including that on the best use of silver, raised a furor during the depression. It was a time of doubt, of searching, and of rapid, confusing change. The gold standard was found wanting; hopes to remonetize silver were anachronistic; and new monetary proposals seemed radical. Out of this conflict emerged experiments to raise prices, stabilize the economy, and test ideas through application. Rejected was the notion that monetary systems must be based on metal to maintain a check on the untrustworthy officials who otherwise would debase the currency and destroy federal credit. This permanently ended the movement.

The silver issue recurred in American politics because its roots ran deeply into the nation's economic and political fabric. Protests subsequent to its demonetization, called the "Crime of '73," were not limited to the West. Many agrarians believed that its restoration to equality with gold would reduce or eliminate the nation's financial and monetary ills. Seemingly, the white metal symbolized the blamelessness of the victims of monometallism. Furthermore, residents of areas remote from large urban centers shared a common desire to resist the power of the city and its people. This fostered a rejection of the East and its gold money, and added impetus to the demands for the white metal.

A complex assortment of motives had contributed to agitation for silver. For some, it was a faith as sacred as religion, for others a means of expressing defiance against the middleman and the mortgage holder, and a potential means to recoup losses produced by the depression. This was as true in the thirties as it had been in the nineties.

In spite of the silver movement of the thirties, the United States finally rejected economic panaceas based on the white metal. While these proposals had long been repudiated in some quarters, they retained their appeal among mineowners and farmers until discredited by the results of large-scale purchases. Thereafter, as other measures to aid agriculture proved effective, faith in the white metal, the poor man's gold, faded into history.

1. George Soule, *Prosperity Decade: From War to Depression, 1917–1929,* Vol. VIII of *The Economic History of the United States,* ed. Henry David *et al.* (9 vols.; New York: Rinehart & Company, Inc., 1947), pp. 234–37.

Bibliography

Unpublished Material

MANUSCRIPT COLLECTIONS

Blood, Henry H. Papers. Utah State Governors File, Utah State Historical Society, Salt Lake City, Utah.

Borah, William E. Collection. Correspondence. Washington State University Library, Pullman, Washington.

.... Papers. Manuscripts Division, Library of Congress, Washington, D.C.

Cannon, Frank J. Papers. State Historical Society of Colorado Library, Denver, Colorado.

Costigan, Edward P. Papers. University of Colorado Library, Boulder, Colorado.

Cutting, Bronson. Papers. Manuscripts Division, Library of Congress, Washington, D.C.

Davis, Norman H. Papers. Manuscripts Division, Library of Congress, Washington, D.C.

Department of Commerce. Records, NCRE–509. National Archives, Social and Economic Branch, Washington, D.C.

Department of the Treasury. Records, NCRD–56. National Archives, Social and Economic Branch, Washington, D.C.

Dern, George H. Papers. Utah State Governors File, Utah State Historical Society, Salt Lake City, Utah.

Johnson, Hiram. Papers. Bancroft Library, University of California, Berkeley, California.

Leavens, Dickenson H. Collection. Manuscripts and publications. University of Colorado Library, Boulder, Colorado.

McCarran, Patrick A. Papers. Nevada State Museum, Carson City, Nevada.

Morgenthau, Henry, Jr. Papers. Franklin D. Roosevelt Library, Hyde Park, New York.

Oddie, Tasker L. Papers. The Huntington Institution Library, San Marino, California.

Pierce, Walter M. Papers. University of Oregon Library, Eugene, Oregon.

Pittman, Key. Papers. Manuscripts Division, Library of Congress, Washington, D.C.

Roosevelt, Franklin D. Papers. Franklin D. Roosevelt Library, Hyde Park, New York.

Thomas, Charles S. Papers. State Historical Society of Colorado, Denver, Colorado.

Thomas, Elbert D. Papers. Franklin D. Roosevelt Library, Hyde Park, New York.

Thomas, Elmer. Papers. Division of Manuscripts, University of Oklahoma Library, Norman, Oklahoma.

Vanderlip, Frank A. Papers. Special Collections, Columbia University Library, New York, New York.

Walsh, Thomas J. Papers. Manuscripts Division, Library of Congress, Washington, D.C.

DIARY AND REMINISCENCES

Morgenthau, Henry, Jr. Diary. Vols. I–XIX. 1933–1936. Henry Morgenthau, Jr., Papers, Franklin D. Roosevelt Library, Hyde Park, New York. (Typewritten.)

Thomas, Elmer. "Forty Years a Legislator." Elmer Thomas Papers, Division of Manuscripts, University of Oklahoma Library, Norman, Oklahoma. (Typewritten.)

.... Letter to author. May 20, 1963.

Wheeler, Burton K. Interview. September 17, 1962. Washington, D.C.

.... Letter to author. September 22, 1961.

DISSERTATIONS

Cooley, Everett L. "Silver Politics in the United States, 1918–1946." Unpublished Ph.D. dissertation, Department of History, University of California, 1951.

Rhodes, Benjamin D. "American Diplomacy and the London Economic Conference." Unpublished Master's thesis, Department of History, University of Colorado, 1961.

Ruetten, Richard T. "Burton K. Wheeler of Montana, A Progressive Between the Wars." Unpublished Ph.D. dissertation, Department of History, University of Oregon, 1961.

Shipps, Jo Ann Barnett. "The Mormons in Politics: The First Hundred Years." Unpublished Ph.D. dissertation, Department of History, University of Colorado, 1965.

Wickens, James F. "Colorado in the Great Depression: A Study of New Deal Policies at the State Level." Unpublished Ph.D. dissertation, Department of Political Science, University of Denver, 1964.

Published Works

PUBLIC DOCUMENTS

Great Britain. *Parliamentary Debates* (Fifth Series). (Commons). Vol. CCLXV (1932).

League of Nations. *Journal of the Monetary and Economic Conference.* Geneva, Switzerland: Documents Service for the Monetary and Economic Conference, 1933.

U.S. Bureau of Mines. *Mineral Facts and Problems.* 1956.

U.S. Bureau of Mines. *Mineral Survey of the United States: 1930.* Part 1.

U.S. Bureau of Mines. *Minerals Yearbook.* 1932–1940.

U.S. *Congressional Directory.* 68th Cong.–74th Cong.

U.S. *Congressional Record.* Vols. LXIV–LXXXIV.

U.S. Department of State. *Foreign Relations of the United States: Diplomatic Papers, 1932.* I.

U.S. Department of State. *Foreign Relations of the United States: Diplomatic Papers, 1933.* I.

U.S. Department of the Treasury. *Annual Report of the Secretary of the Treasury on the State of Finances.* 1934–1938.

U.S. Geological Survey. *Mineral Resources of the United States: 1920.* Part 1.

U.S. House of Representatives, Committee on Coinage, Weights and Measures. *Hearings, The Effects of Low Silver.* 72d Cong., 1st Sess., 1932.

U.S. House of Representatives, Committee on Coinage, Weights and Measures. *Hearings, Silver Money.* 72d Cong., 2d Sess., 1933.

U.S. House of Representatives, Committee on Coinage, Weights and Measures. *Report, Exchange of Agricultural Surpluses for Silver.* Report No. 992, 73d Cong., 2d Sess., 1934.

U.S. Senate, Commission of Gold and Silver Inquiry. *Progress Report of Senate Commission of Gold and Silver Inquiry.* Document No. 38, 68th Cong., 1st Sess., 1924.

U.S. Senate, Committee on Agriculture and Forestry. *Report, Encourage Sale of American Agricultural Surplus Products Abroad; To Provide Payment Therefor in Silver, and to Provide for Purchase of Silver.* Report No. 697, 73d Cong., 2d Sess., 1934.

U.S. Senate, Committee on Agriculture and Forestry. *Report, Relieve the Existing National Economic Emergency by Increasing Agricultural Purchasing Power.* Report No. 16, 73d Cong., 1st Sess., 1933.

U.S. Senate, Committee on Agriculture and Forestry. *Report, Repeal of Sections 6, 7, and 8 of the Silver Purchase Act of 1934.* Report No. 1911, 74th Cong., 1st Sess., 1935.

U.S. Senate, Committee on Banking and Currency. *Report, Currency Amendment to the Farm Relief Bill.* Report No. 40, 73d Cong., 1st Sess., 1933.

U.S. Senate, Committee on Foreign Relations. *Hearings, Commercial Relations with China.* 71st Cong., 2d Sess., 1930.

U.S. Senate. *Hoarders of Silver.* Document No. 173, 73d Cong., 2d Sess., 1934.

U.S. Senate. *Silver and the Foreign Debt Payments.* Document No. 8, 73d Cong., 1st Sess., 1933.

U.S. *Statutes at Large.* Vols. XL–LXXVII.

DIARIES, MEMOIRS, PUBLIC
PAPERS, AND BIOGRAPHIES

Acheson, Dean G. *Morning and Noon*. Boston: Houghton Mifflin Company, 1965.

Burns, James MacGregor. *Roosevelt: The Lion and the Fox*. New York: Harcourt, Brace and Company, 1956.

Cannon, Frank J., and O'Higgins, Harvey J. *Under the Prophet in Utah*. Boston: The C. M. Clark Publishing Company, 1911.

Capper, Arthur. *The Agricultural Bloc*. New York: Harcourt, Brace and Company, 1922.

Coletta, Paolo E. *William Jennings Bryan*, Vol. I. *Political Evangelist, 1860–1908*. Lincoln, Nebraska: University of Nebraska Press, 1964.

Coughlin, Charles E. *The New Deal in Money*. Royal Oak, Michigan: Radio League of the Little Flower, 1933.

Eccles, Marriner S. *Beckoning Frontiers: Public and Personal Recollections*. New York: Alfred A. Knopf, 1951.

Feis, Herbert. *1933, Characters in Crisis*. Boston: Little, Brown and Company, 1966.

Fite, Gilbert C. *George N. Peek and the Fight for Farm Parity*. Norman, Oklahoma: University of Oklahoma Press, 1954.

Glad, Paul W. *The Trumpet Soundeth: William Jennings Bryan and his Democracy, 1896–1912*. Lincoln, Nebraska: University of Nebraska Press, 1960.

Handlin, Oscar. *Al Smith and His America*. Boston: Little, Brown and Company, 1958.

Hoover, Herbert C. *The Memoirs of Herbert Hoover*. Vol. III. *The Great Depression, 1929–1941*. New York: The Macmillan Company, 1952.

Hull, Cordell. *The Memoirs of Cordell Hull*. 2 vols. New York: The Macmillan Company, 1948.

Ickes, Harold L. *The Secret Diary of Harold L. Ickes*. Vol. I. *The First Thousand Days, 1933–1936*. New York: Simon and Schuster, 1953.

169

Israel, Fred L. *Nevada's Key Pittman.* Lincoln, Nebraska: University of Nebraska Press, 1963.

Johnson, Claudius O. *Borah of Idaho.* New York: Longmans, Green and Company, 1936.

Jones, Jesse H., with Angly, Edward. *Fifty Billion Dollars: My Thirteen Years with the RFC (1932–1945).* New York: The Macmillan Company, 1951.

Keating, Edward. *The Gentleman from Colorado, a Memoir.* Denver, Colorado: Sage Books, 1964.

Levine, Lawrence W. *Defender of the Faith: William Jennings Bryan, The Last Decade, 1915–1925.* New York: Oxford University Press, 1965.

Linebarger, Paul Myron W. *The Gospel of Chung Shan.* Paris: Brenatano's, 1932.

Merrill, Milton R. *Reed Smoot, Utah Politician.* (Monograph Series, Vol. I, No. 2.) Logan, Utah: Utah State University Press, April, 1953.

Moley, Raymond I. *After Seven Years.* New York: Harper and Brothers, 1939.

-----------, *The First New Deal.* New York: Harcourt, Brace and World, Inc., 1966.

Mullen, Arthur F. *Western Democrat.* New York: W. Funk, Inc., 1940.

Rollins, Alfred B., Jr. *Roosevelt and Howe.* New York: Alfred A. Knopf, 1962.

Roosevelt, Elliott (ed.). *F. D. R., His Personal Letters, 1928–1945.* 4 vols. New York: Duell, Sloan & Pearce, 1947–1950.

Rosenman, Samuel I. (ed.). *The Public Papers and Addresses of Franklin D. Roosevelt.* Vol. II. *The Year of Crisis 1933.* New York: Random House, 1938.

Sparks, George F. (ed.). *A Many Colored Toga, the Diary of Henry Fountain Ashurst.* Tuscon, Arizona: University of Arizona Press, 1962.

Thomas, Sewell. *Silhouettes of Charles S. Thomas.* Caldwell, Idaho: The Caxton Printers, Ltd., 1959.

Tugwell, Rexford G. *The Democratic Roosevelt.* Garden City, New York: Doubleday, Doran & Company, 1957.

Tull, Charles J. *Father Coughlin and the New Deal.* Syracuse, New York: Syracuse University Press, 1965.

Warburg, James P. *The Long Road Home.* Garden City, New York: Doubleday & Company, Inc., 1964.

⸺. *The Money Muddle.* New York: Alfred A. Knopf, 1934.

Wheeler, Burton K., with Healy, Paul F. *Yankee from the West.* Garden City, New York: Doubleday & Company, Inc., 1962.

MONOGRAPHS

Allen, G. C., and Donnethrone, Audrey G. *Western Enterprise in Far Eastern Economic Development: China and Japan.* New York: The Macmillan Company, 1954.

Arrington, Leonard J. *The Changing Economic Structure of the Mountain West, 1850–1950.* (Monograph Series, Vol. x, No. 3.) Logan, Utah: Utah State University Press, June, 1963.

Barger, Harold, and Schurr, Sam H. *The Mining Industries, 1899–1939: A Study of Output, Employment and Productivity.* New York: National Bureau of Economic Research, Inc., 1944.

Bassett, Reginald. *Nineteen Thirty-One: Political Crisis.* London: The Macmillan Company, 1938.

Bernstein, Marvin D. *The Mexican Mining Industry, 1890–1950.* Albany, New York: State University of New York, 1965.

Blum, John M. *From the Morgenthau Diaries.* Vol. i. *Years of Crisis, 1928–1938.* Boston: Houghton Mifflin Company, 1959.

Crawford, Arthur Whipple. *Monetary Management Under the New Deal.* Washington: American Council on Public Affairs, 1940.

Donnelly, Thomas C. (ed.). *Rocky Mountain Politics.* Albuquerque, New Mexico: University of New Mexico Press, 1940.

Everest, Allan Seymour. *Morgenthau, the New Deal, and Silver; A Story of Pressure Politics.* New York: King's Crown Press, 1950.

Friedman, Milton, and Schwartz, Anna Jacobson. *A Monetary*

History of the United States, 1867–1960. Princeton, New Jersey: Princeton University Press, 1963.

Fusfeld, Daniel R. *The Economic Thought of Franklin D. Roosevelt and the Origins of the New Deal.* New York: Columbia University Press, 1956.

Garnsey, Morris E. *America's New Frontier: The Mountain West.* New York: Alfred A. Knopf, 1950.

Glad, Paul W. *McKinley, Bryan and the People.* Philadelphia: J. B. Lippincott Company, 1964.

Greever, William S. *The Bonanza West: The Story of the Western Mining Rushes, 1848–1900.* Norman, Oklahoma: University of Oklahoma Press, 1963.

Hicks, John D. *The Populist Revolt: A History of the Farmers' Alliance and the People's Party.* Minneapolis, Minnesota: University of Minnesota Press, 1931.

Hollon, W. Eugene. *The Southwest: Old and New.* New York: Alfred A. Knopf, 1961.

Jonas, Frank H. (ed.). *Western Politics.* Salt Lake City, Utah: University of Utah Press, 1961.

Leavens, Dickenson H. *Silver Money.* Bloomington, Indiana: Principia Press, Inc., 1939.

Leong, Y. S. *Silver: An Analysis of the Factors Affecting Its Price.* Washington: The Brookings Institution, 1933.

Leuchtenburg, William E. *Franklin D. Roosevelt and the New Deal, 1932–1940.* A volume in the New American Nation Series, edited by Henry Steele Commager and Richard B. Morris. New York: Harper, Row and Company, 1963.

Lin, Wei-Ying. *China Under Depreciated Silver, 1926–1931.* Shanghai: The Commercial Press, 1935.

————— *The New Monetary System of China: A Personal Interpretation.* Chicago: The University of Chicago Press, 1936.

Lindley, Ernest K. *The Roosevelt Revolution, First Phase.* New York: The Viking Press, 1933.

Linebarger, Paul Myron Anthony. *Government in Republican China.* New York: McGraw Hill Book Company, 1938.

Lippmann, Walter. *Interpretations, 1933–1935.* New York: The Macmillan Company, 1936.

McCoy, Donald R. *Angry Voices: Left-of-center Politics in the New Deal Era.* Lawrence, Kansas: University of Kansas Press, 1958.

McCune, Wesley. *Farm Bloc.* Garden City, New York: Doubleday, Doran and Company, 1943.

Marcosson, Isaac F. *Metal Magic: The Story of American Smelting and Refining Company.* New York: Farrar, Straus and Company, 1949.

Mitchell, Broadus. *Depression Decade: From New Era Through New Deal, 1929–1941* Vol. IX of *The Economic History of the United States,* edited by Henry David *et al.* New York: Rinehart and Company, Inc., 1947.

Mowry, George E. *The Urban Nation, 1920–1960.* New York: Hill and Wang, 1965.

Nussbaum, Arthur. *A History of the Dollar.* New York: Columbia University Press, 1957.

Ostrander, Gilman M. *Nevada, The Great Rotten Borough, 1859–1964.* New York: Alfred A. Knopf, 1966.

Paris, James Daniel. *Monetary Policies of the United States, 1932–1938.* New York: Columbia University Press, 1938.

Paul, Rodman W. *Mining Frontiers of the Far West, 1848–1880.* New York: Holt, Rinehart and Winston, 1963.

Pomeroy, Earl M. *The Pacific Slope: A History of California, Oregon, Washington, Idaho, Utah, and Nevada.* New York: Alfred A. Knopf, 1965.

Rauch, Basil. *The History of the New Deal 1933–1938.* New York: Creative Age Press, Inc., 1944.

Reeve, Joseph E. *Monetary Reform Movements: A Survey of Recent Plans and Panaceas.* Washington: American Council on Public Affairs, 1943.

Rickard, Thomas A. *The History of American Mining.* New York: McGraw-Hill Book Company, 1932.

Saloutos, Theodore and Hicks, John D. *Agricultural Discontent in the Middle West, 1900–1939.* Madison, Wisconsin: University of Wisconsin Press, 1951.

Schlesinger, Arthur M., Jr. *The Age of Roosevelt.* Vol. I: *The Crisis of the Old Order.* Vol. II: *The Coming of the New*

Deal. Vol. III: *The Politics of Upheaval.* Boston: Houghton Mifflin Company, 1957–1960.

Shover, John L. *Cornbelt Rebellion: The Farmers' Holiday Association.* Urbana, Illinois: University of Illinois Press, 1965.

Soule, George. *Prosperity Decade: From War to Depression, 1917–1929.* Vol. VIII of *The Economic History of the United States,* edited by Henry David *et al.* New York: Rinehart & Company, Inc., 1947.

Thomas, Elmer. *Financial Engineering.* Washington: privately published, 1953.

Wallace, Henry A. *New Frontiers.* New York: Reynal & Hitchcock, 1934.

Westerfield, Ray B. *Our Silver Debacle.* New York: The Ronald Press, 1936.

Woofter, T. J., Jr., and Winston, Ellen. *Seven Lean Years.* Chapel Hill, North Carolina: University of North Carolina Press, 1939.

ARTICLES

Arrington, Leonard J. "Abundance from the Earth: The Beginnings of Commercial Mining in Utah," *Utah Historical Quarterly,* XXXI (Summer, 1963), 192–219.

Baruch, Bernard M. "The Dangers of Inflation," *Saturday Evening Post,* CCVI (November 25, 1933), 5–7, 84–87.

Bell, Elliott V. "The Silver Fiasco," *Current History,* XLIII (January, 1936), 473–78.

Bratter, Herbert M. "The Committee for the Nation: A Case History in Monetary Propaganda," *The Journal of Political Economy,* XLIX (August, 1941), 531–53.

.... "The Silver Episode, I," *The Journal of Political Economy,* XLVI (October, 1938), 609–52.

.... "The Silver Episode, II," *The Journal of Political Economy,* XLVI (December, 1938), 802–37.

.... "Silver, Some Fundamentals," *The Journal of Political Economy,* XXXIX (June, 1931), 21–68.

Brownell, Francis H. "Silver, Its Future as Money," *The North American Review,* CCXXXIII (March, 1932), 234–42.

Carothers, Neil. "Silver—A Senate Racket," *The North American Review,* CCXXXIII (January, 1932), 4–15.

Corey, Herbert. "The Silver Swindle," *The American Mercury,* XLVIII (September, 1939), 18–25.

Crider, John H. "Cross of Silver," *The North American Review,* CCXLV (June, 1938), 280–91.

"Doing Something for Silver," *Fortune,* XII (July, 1935), 74–88.

Ellison, Herbert B. "China Dethrones Silver," *Foreign Affairs,* XIV (January, 1936), 334–39.

.... "The Silver Problem," *Foreign Affairs,* IX (April, 1931), 441–56.

.... "Uncle Sam, The Silver King," *The Atlantic Monthly,* CLX (September, 1937), 363–65.

Fisher, Irving. "Reflation and Deflation," *The Annals of the American Academy of Political and Social Science,* CLXXI (January, 1934), 127–31.

Froman, A. Lewis. "Bimetallism—Reconsidered in the Light of Recent Developments," *The American Economic Review,* XXVI (March, 1936), 53–61.

Graham, Frank D. "The Fall in the Value of Silver and Its Consequences," *The Journal of Political Economy,* XXXIX (August, 1931), 425–70.

Herring, E. Pendleton. "Second Session of the Seventy-Third Congress, January 3, 1934 to June 18, 1934," *American Political Science Review,* XXVIII (October, 1934), 852–66.

Jonas, Frank H. "The Third Man in Utah Politics," *Utah Academy of Science, Arts, and Letters, Proceedings,* XXXVIII (1960), 115–21.

Kent, Fred I. "The Mystery of the Gold Standard," *The Literary Digest,* CXVI (July, 1933), 5–7, 32–33.

Lawrence, Joseph Stagg. "The Unimportance of Silver," *World's Work,* LX (August, 1931), 21–25, 66–67.

Leavens, Dickenson H. "American Silver Policy and China," *Harvard Business Review,* XIV (Autumn, 1935), 45–58.

175

.... "Silver and the Business Depression," *Harvard Business Review,* IX (April, 1931), 330–38.

Lisman, F. J. "Silver, Sentiment and Politics," *Baron's,* XII (May 23, 1932), 5.

Mazur, Paul M. "The Gold Crisis: Its Causes and Significance," *Current History,* XXXV (November, 1931), 167–72.

Nevins, Allan. "Echoes of Two Historic Money Battles," *New York Times Magazine,* LXXXIII (December 17, 1933), 4–5.

Nichols, Jeanette P. "Roosevelt's Monetary Diplomacy in 1933," *The American Historical Review,* LVI (January, 1951), 295–317.

.... "Silver Inflation and the Senate in 1933," *The Social Studies,* XXV (January, 1934), 12–18.

Pell, Herbert C. "Free Silver," *The North American Review,* CCXXXVII (March, 1934), 198–202.

Perkins, Van L. "The AAA and the Politics of Agriculture: Agricultural Policy Formulation in the Fall of 1933," *Agricultural History,* XXXIX (October, 1965), 220–29.

Polenberg, Richard. "The National Committee to Uphold Constitutional Government, 1937–1941," *The Journal of American History,* LII (December, 1965), 582–98.

Porter, Sylvia F. "Uncle Sam's Silver Scandal," *Reader's Digest,* XXXVI (May, 1940), 77–80.

Shover, John L. "The Penny-Auction Rebellion," *The American West,* II (Fall, 1965), 64–72.

.... "Populism in the Nineteen-Thirties: The Battle for the AAA," *Agricultural History,* XXXIX (January, 1965), 17–24.

Thomas, Charles S. "The Unimportance of Silver—a Reply," U.S., *Congressional Record,* 72d Cong., 1st Sess., 1931, LXXV, Part 1 (December 15, 1931), 514–17.

Thomas, Elmer. "Money and Its Management," *The Annals of the American Academy of Political and Social Science,* CLXXI (January, 1934), 132–37.

Tuck, Edward. "Honest Inflation," *Scribner's Magazine,* XCV (January, 1934), 9–14.

Wheeler, Burton K. "The Silver Lining," *Liberty,* IX (October, 1932), 12–18.

White, Owen P. "The Silver Mirage," *Collier's*, XCVI (July 6, 1935), 12–13, 60–61.
Willis, H. Parker. "Silver," *The New Republic*, LXVI (March 11, 1931), 92–94.

NEWSPAPERS

Boston Evening News, Clippings,* 1933–1934.
Boston Evening Transcript, Clippings,* 1933–1934.
Boston Herald, Clippings,* 1933.
Boston Post, Clippings,* 1933.
Commercial and Financial Chronicle (New York), 1933–1934.
The Denver Post, 1931–1935.
Idaho Daily Statesman (Boise), 1933–1934.
Nevada State Journal (Reno), 1934.
New York Herald-Tribune, Clippings,* 1933–1934.
New York Times, 1926–1935.
Philadelphia Herald-Inquirer, Clippings,* 1933.
Rocky Mountain News (Denver), 1931–1935.
Salt Lake Tribune, 1932–1934.
San Francisco Examiner, 1933.
The Times (London), 1932–1933.

SERIAL PUBLICATIONS

Engineering and Mining Journal. Vols. CXXII–CXXXII. New York: McGraw-Hill Publishing Co., 1926–1931.
Engineering and Mining Journal-Press. Vols. CXIII–CX. New York: McGraw-Hill Publishing Co., 1922–1926.
Mines Register. Vol. XIX. New York: Mines Publications, Inc., 1937.

---

*Leavens, Dickenson H. Collection. University of Colorado Library, Boulder, Colorado.

BIBLIOGRAPHY

Mining Yearbook. Vols. I–III. Denver, Colorado: Colorado Mining Association, 1933–1936.

Money. Vol. I. Denver, Colorado: Money Publishing Co., 1932.

Index

Adams, Alva B., 5, 50, 62, 121, 124, 128, 142–143
Adams, William H., 49
Agitation, silver: 3, 37, 47–51, 55–58, 61, 63, 77, 82, 84, 97, 101, 104, 110, 112, 117 n60, 119–120, 124, 130, 139, 143–145, 150; and money issue, 1; in seventies, nineties, twenties, 2; opposition to, articles written in 1931, 14; opposition to, and silverite response, 15; reemerging in 1931, 17; opposition during International Chamber of Commerce convention, 24; prospects, 1931, 25; support from commodity growers, 28; urged by Pittman, 28–29; complicated by issue's political legacy, 30; proponents divided, 33; western drives, 41; loan to China, 44; drive for loan ended, 46; Cannon begins bimetallism drive, 46; declined in 1932, 50; at House Coinage Committee hearings, 56; encouraged by Borah, 58; demanded by partisans, 62; and higher world prices, 92; bimetallism drive counterproductive, 91; unaffected by publicity on silver speculation, 125; increases pressure on FDR to initiate silver legislation, 122; proponents' varied reactions to Silver Purchase Act, 131; deeply rooted and complexly motivated, 163–164
Agricultural Adjustment Act, 63, 87, 97, 160
Agricultural distress: 31, 56, 65, 69, 99, 115 n10, 159; blamed on money, 1; causes farmers to support silver interests, 5; and money supply, 17; fosters union with silverites, 61; recurrence after mid-

1933, 83; proposal for reduction of surpluses and retention of foreign markets, 121–122; easing in 1935 ended rural agitation, 146
Agricultural Surpluses Exchange Board, 119, 128
Agriculture and Forestry, U.S. Senate Committee on, 63, 65, 98, 121, 124
American Farm Bureau Federation, 46
American Federation of Labor, 9
American Metal Company, 51 n8, 56
American Mining Congress, 29
American Silver Producers' Association: 7, 42, 57; purpose, leadership, 8; conflicts within, 9; ineffectiveness, 10; favors limited purchase legislation, 32
American Smelting and Refining Company, 7, 12, 29, 46, 56
Anaconda Copper Mining Co., 7, 31, 51 n8
Ashurst, Henry F., 60–62, 114
Aspen, Colorado, 41

Baruch, Bernard: 35, 46; opposes inflation, 102
Bank of the United States, 105
Banking and Currency, U.S. Senate Committee on, 32–33, 65, 67, 116 n48, 120, 130
Bimetallic Association, 46, 49–50
Bimetallism: 15, 28–30, 46–51, 55, 60, 62–64, 68, 70 n9, 75, 77, 109, 119, 126, 132; defended by C. S. Thomas, 16; endorsed by John R. Commons, 17; feared as political issue, 30; eastern press opposed, 31; tabled by Senate, 60; mandatory legislation predicted by Pittman, 84; advocates oppose

179

SPO, Carson City, Nevada, 1969